Women and Work

Mapping Social Reproduction Theory

Series editors Tithi Bhattacharya, Professor of South Asian History and the Director of Global Studies at Purdue University; and Susan Ferguson, Associate Professor, Faculty of Liberal Arts, Wilfrid Laurier University

Capitalism is a system of exploitation and oppression. This series uses the insights of Social Reproduction Theory to deepen our understanding of the intimacy of that relationship, and the contradictions within it, past and present. The books include empirical investigations of the ways in which social oppressions of race, sexuality, ability, gender and more inhabit, shape and are shaped by the processes of creating labour power for capital. The books engage a critical exploration of Social Reproduction, enjoining debates about the theoretical and political tools required to challenge capitalism today.

Also available

Social Reproduction Theory:
Remapping Class, Recentering Oppression
Edited by Tithi Bhattacharya

Women and Work

Feminism, Labour, and Social Reproduction

Susan Ferguson

First published 2020 by Pluto Press
345 Archway Road, London N6 5AA

www.plutobooks.com

British Library Cataloguing in Publication Data
A catalogue record for this book is available from the British Library

ISBN   978 0 7453 3872 9   Hardback
ISBN   978 0 7453 3871 2   Paperback
ISBN   978 1 7868 0427 3   PDF eBook
ISBN   978 1 7868 0429 7   Kindle eBook
ISBN   978 1 7868 0428 0   EPUB eBook

This book is printed on paper suitable for recycling and made from fully
managed and sustained forest sources. Logging, pulping and manufacturing
processes are expected to conform to the environmental standards of the
country of origin.

Typeset by Stanford DTP Services, Northampton, England

Simultaneously printed in the United Kingdom and United States of America

For David.

Contents

Acknowledgements

The immediate inspiration for this book came from a chapter I was asked to contribute to *The Bloomsbury Handbook of 21st-Century Feminist Theory*. So my first thank you is to Robin Truth Goodman, that book's editor, for nudging me to figure out that there was a story to tell about feminist thinking about labour. But it would take more than 6500 words to do it greater justice. I want to thank David Shulman at Pluto for picking up on my enthusiasm for the book, and understanding as I lay aside (for now) a project on childhood and capitalism I have also planned with Pluto. I am grateful for his guidance through the proposal process and beyond, and throughout the launch of the Social Reproduction Theory book series. Neda Tehrani at Pluto has also been a pleasure to work with, and her feedback reassuring and valuable. I have worked through some of the ideas in the book at various Historical Materialism conferences, and am especially grateful to my co-organizers of the London HM Marxist Feminist stream for ensuring space is carved out every year to keep these and other socialist feminist discussions alive. I also want to acknowledge the Faculty of Liberal Arts at Wilfrid Laurier University for support given to my research over the years, this last year especially while I was on sabbatical leave.

I have been inspired and supported by many friends, colleagues, comrades, and family members. To single out a few: Alan Sears, for our fun and far-ranging chats at Page One that helped shaped my thinking; I also want to thank Alan along with James Cairns for their always thoughtful, probing feedback on earlier chapters; Karley Doucette for our discussions about socialist feminism, the *Handmaid's Tale*, and the papers we heard at the Marxist Institute's Summer School in Albany; Mary-Jo Nadeau for lending me her MA thesis and for her unflagging political activism and wisdom; Sam Ferguson, one of my amazing sons, for his insightful comments on early chapters, as well as for patiently seeing me through computer and internet transitions and glitches; my other amazing sons, Liam and Adam McNally, and my sisters, Anne and Karen, for their love and support; Anne gets honourable mention for feeding me delicious dinners at critical junctures as my deadline approached and no one was home to cook for me; and a big thank you to Tithi Bhattacharya, who has done so much to advance and publicize the ideas and political commitments of social reproduction feminism over the past decade, for her valuable feedback on and enthusiasm for this book, as well as for our ongoing collaboration on this book series and other projects.

Finally, I don't have the words to adequately thank David McNally. I can only say that without him, this book would not have been written. Throughout its writing, despite huge changes in our lives as we uprooted and moved from Toronto to Houston, he gave unfailingly of his time, insight and wisdom, his love and support. Thank you sweetie.

Introduction

When Hillary Clinton won the Democratic presidential nomination in July 2016, it was widely seen as a triumph for feminism. Clinton had climbed up the patriarchal ladder in the 1970s and 1980s, smashing glass ceilings along the way to become a wealthy lawyer, New York state senator, and eventually US Secretary of State in the Obama administration. She seemed the very picture of a working woman who had made it in a man's world. As former Texas senator Wendy Davis told the Democratic Party's women's caucus at the time, "We have never, ever had someone who has walked in our shoes, we have never had someone who understands what it means to be a woman in America, and we have never had the kind of champion that we are going to have in Hillary Clinton."[1]

Alas, Clinton didn't fare as well in her next job interview. She lost the contest for president of the United States to a man. Not just to any man, but to one notoriously sexist Donald Trump. It looked like Americans would accept almost anything to keep a woman out of the White House. Just as feminism propelled Clinton forward, her supporters lamented, anti-feminism stopped her in her tracks.

Yet, a few months later, the wind was fully in feminism's sails, albeit blowing in a different direction. In January 2017, hundreds of thousands marched through city streets around the world, waving placards with angry, witty quips at Trump's outrageously loutish behaviour and warning that feminism's hard-fought gains will not be easily dismantled. Then on March 8, International Women's Day (IWD), they took to the streets again responding to a call to resist not only "Trump and his misogynist policies, but also ... the conditions that produced Trump, namely the decades long economic inequality, racial and sexual violence, and imperial wars abroad."[2]

This was a different—but not entirely new—direction for feminist politics. Socialist feminists who organized international Women's Strikes to coordinate with IWD demonstrations did what feminists in Latin America, Italy, and Poland had been doing in recent years, and what feminists have done during upsurges of struggle throughout history: they called on women to strike—to walk off their waged and unwaged jobs, and to join with anti-racist, queer, trans, Indigenous activists, and others in demanding that people's environmental, social, economic, and reproductive needs be met. In the United States, organizers call the movement Feminism for the 99%.[3] In Argentina, it is called "popular feminism," and described as a struggle based on "a situated, class-based feminism that seeks to grow in relation to emancipatory political projects."[4] Such resistance looks very different from vying for a seat in a boardroom or the oval office for a good reason: these feminists aim not to break into a man's world, but to change that world by collectively refusing the work that upholds it.

This book is about the different ways in which feminists have understood work, and women's work in particular, in relation to questions of freedom and oppression. Work becomes an issue for women, I propose in Chapter 1, precisely because the emergence of capitalism makes it one. That is, capitalism develops only by trapping and distilling the generalized capacity of humans to labour. But it does so not simply—or even primarily—by feeding off the productive potential of waged labourers. It does so equally by reorganizing and devaluing all of people's life-making activities, most of which have been the tasks assigned to women. The book thus spans the four centuries of capitalism's existence. And it considers feminist positions associated with numerous political traditions—from 1790s radical democracy through nineteenth-century utopian socialist communitarianism and African American women's club movement feminism to the international Wages for Housework campaign and today's Feminism for the 99% project. It traces feminist theories of labour throughout this history, conceptualizing them along three broad trajectories in order to come to terms with why and how feminists have disagreed about women's work. Those trajectories are: *equality, critical equality,* and *social reproduction* feminisms.

But more than just a mapping of the past to present, the ensuing chapters also construct an argument about the way forward for those of us interested in building a broad-based, pluralist socialist movement. I propose that the perspective which has historically dominated socialist feminism, *critical equality feminism,* has limited the scope and potential of socialist feminism to develop the sort of inclusive working class politics needed to move beyond the ravages of capitalism. I also explain how and why *social reproduction feminism,* on the other hand, develops a theory of work that broadens our understanding of class and class struggle. This closer look at social reproduction feminism occurs in the last three

chapters of the book. There, I consider various formulations of that theoretical approach, and seek to explain how certain recent developments in
that trajectory succeed in showing us what it will take to create a society
in which work is an expression of freedom, not oppression.

PART I: THREE TRAJECTORIES

Equality feminism takes root in the late eighteenth-century writings of
Mary Wollstonecraft and other radical democratic feminists, whose
work I discuss in Chapter 2. As it develops into a more coherent
framework, equality feminism incorporates a sustained critique of the
gender division of labour: women's relegation to (difficult, isolated, and
undervalued) work enforces their vulnerability to the arbitrary rule of
husbands and fathers while breeding dependence on men. Freedom is
thus to be found in their independence from men—which is attained,
in large part, through access to waged work (and the education required
for decent employment). This approach, I suggest, sits squarely in the
rational-humanist tradition of critique, the same tradition of moral philosophy on which pre-modern European feminists drew.

Social reproduction feminism also begins with troubling the gender
division of labour. In Chapter 3 I show how early nineteenth-century
utopian socialists Anna Wheeler and William Thompson move beyond
moral philosophical traditions. They do so by beginning to develop a
political-economic analysis of women's work in the home. According to
Wheeler and Thompson, women are oppressed not simply because they
are excluded from waged labour and forced to be housewives. Rather,
their oppression is a question of how and why such labour is devalued in
the first instance, which these utopian socialists assess by theorizing its
contribution to overall social wealth. Their contribution lays the foundation for a new perspective: social reproduction feminism directs our
attention to the interaction between unpaid and paid labour, positioning
these as different-but-equally-essential parts of the same overall (capitalist) system. As such, it sees the division and ongoing relation between
the two forms of labour, not the nature of gendered labour, as the central
feminist problem. It follows then that women's emancipation hinges on
the radical reorganization and reimagining of the whole world of work.
It also follows that capitalism will not be overturned unless women's
oppression is addressed as part of the class struggle.

Chapter 3 also introduces the *critical equality feminist* trajectory through the mid-nineteenth-century writings of French socialist feminist Flora Tristan. This perspective shares social reproduction feminism's critique of capitalism's separation of productive from reproductive work, but it does so without elaborating a political-economic analysis of unpaid women's work. Instead, it analyzes, more one-sidedly, the gender division of labour, adopting the rational-humanist framework of equality feminism that attributes women's oppression to their dependence on men, also suggesting that waged work will secure women's independence from men. Critical equality feminism departs from equality feminism, however, in its claim that waged work for women is but a first step in a wider freedom project: because women are excluded from socially productive work in capitalist societies, they cannot be free until capitalism too is overturned. Women's workforce participation therefore has a further rationale: along with being released from men's subjugation, women workers fortify the class struggle against capitalism.

Critical equality feminism thus combines two forms of analysis: a rational-humanist critique of women's unpaid labour and a political-economic critique of waged labour. August Bebel and Friedrich Engels elaborate and sanction this hybrid approach as the socialist movement's more-or-less official response to "the woman question" for decades to come. This approach, I argue in Chapter 4, explains why socialist feminism tends toward theoretical dualism (the tendency to conceive patriarchal and capitalist powers as two distinct sets of social relations). Such theoretical dualism, as critics have long pointed out, engenders an equally dualist, and flawed, political perspective in which the specifically *feminist* struggle is distinct from—and added on to—the class struggle: women fight (men or the state) for their independence from men; workers fight bosses for control over their labour power. It also can promote a class reductionist political perspective: because capitalism must be ended before women can be free, the feminist struggle can always be deferred in the name of building working class unity.

Chapter 4 looks as well at two socialist feminists, revolutionaries Clara Zetkin and Alexandra Kollontai, who argue valiantly against such dualist and class reductionist politics.[5] Each has considerable insight into the importance of the feminist struggle for socialism. But insofar as they embrace a critical equality feminist perspective on women's labour, they fail to theorize their way out of the confusions introduced by the hybrid approach. That perspective correctly points to the historical co-emergence of capitalist waged labour and unpaid domestic labour, but it does not theorize any *systemic* or necessary relation between them. It lacks a theory of their interdependency. As a result, critical equality feminism lacks the basis from which to argue that feminist and worker struggles are two different parts of the same class struggle.

Part I closes with a discussion of the traditions of anti-racist feminism which have embraced and moved beyond the three trajectories I've outlined. As early as the 1820s, those writing about black women's experiences called attention to the more complex realities not just of women's lives but of women's work, and of domestic labour in particular. I take a close look at Claudia Jones, an African American feminist Communist Party USA member in the 1940s and 1950s. Her insights about the integrated nature of racial, gender, and class oppression across realms of waged and unwaged labour gesture toward a social reproduction feminism perspective. Unfortunately, white socialist feminists who go on to develop that perspective fail to take note.

PART II: SOCIAL REPRODUCTION FEMINISM

Social reproduction feminism, I hope this book convinces readers, offers a way out of the theoretical conundrums that have characterized the socialist feminism tradition. It does so, however, only after sorting through a few muddles of its own. Its central innovation is the theorization of the feminist struggle *as* an anti-capitalist struggle, a class struggle. While critical equality feminism asserts that women's oppression ends only when capitalism is overturned, social reproduction feminism grapples with the logic behind that claim.

Chapter 6 considers several notable contributors to this trajectory, Mary Inman, Margaret Benston, Sheila Rowbotham, and the international Wages for Housework campaign theorists, Silvia Federici, Maria Dalla Costa, and Selma James. I chose these contributors because they nicely represent the two-sided development of the trajectory: the interpretation of social reproductive labour as capitalistically productive (that is, value-producing) labour, on the one hand, or as capitalistically unproductive (use value-producing only), on the other. While this may appear to be an outdated debate (those familiar with socialist feminism's history will sigh, no doubt, about revisiting the Domestic Labour Debate), I argue that it is still highly relevant: how feminists understand unpaid domestic labour has determined the sort of political strategy they embrace, both in the 1970s and today.

At the same time, I recognize that splitting the theoretical hairs of Marxian value theory is both an arcane and abstract undertaking, and so I have reserved the heavy lifting for the first half of Chapter 8. Those disinclined to dig in are invited to skip to the second half of that chapter! Chapter 6 looks at the strengths and weaknesses of social reproduction feminism from the 1940s through to the 1970s, contrasting it to both Betty Friedan's liberal equality feminism and the radical feminism of the New York Redstockings group among others. I argue that despite its insights, social reproduction feminism in this era places too much determinative weight on unpaid housework—a move that leaves it open to the same sort of tendencies we see in critical equality feminism, theoretical dualism, and class reductionism.

As a result, and like the other trajectories, social reproduction feminism is challenged to theorize labour in ways that can explain oppressions other than gender. I revisit anti-racist feminism in Chapter 7 through a discussion of the work of the Combahee River Collective and Angela Davis. Here, I propose that the most promising response to the black feminist call for an analysis and politics that captures the integral relation of class and social oppressions can be found in today's renewed social reproduction feminism. That renewal follows Lise Vogel in dislodging unpaid housework from the centre of its analysis and insisting instead on the necessary-but-contradictory relation of social reproductive to productive work. In unlocking the possibility of critically integrating the arguments black feminists have long been making about women's social reproductive work, Vogel enabled social reproduction feminism to move beyond its own theoretical obfuscations.

This leads me to Chapter 8, where I address the question of value theory as it has been debated by the two schools of thought within social reproduction feminism. The point of that discussion is to explain how and why those schools—one associated with the autonomist Marxist understanding of value production, the other adhering closely to Marx's explanation of value in *Capital*—advocate distinct political strategies. While the former emphasizes the need to move outside capitalism and develop revolutionary commons through which people learn new ways of reproducing themselves and their worlds, the other looks to building mass movements capable of breaking the system from within. These are not mutually exclusive strategies of course, nor should they be. But, as I try to show, the latter is absolutely essential, but not something that is the necessary or logical conclusion of autonomist Marxist feminism.

FINAL THOUGHTS

Clearly, a book that surveys centuries of feminist thinking has certain limitations. Most notably, it leaves much out. In choosing texts to highlight, I relied on my sense of those who contributed either genuinely theoretical innovations or who best exemplified theoretical trends. Because my choices are guided by what historians consider a "feminist canon," this is a story of Euro-American (mostly British-American) feminism. Telling the stories of Indigenous, Indian, South American, African, Australian, Mid-Eastern, and Asian feminist theories of labour would be better done by others more expert on those traditions. Yet, as a book about how women's work has been conceptualized in capitalist societies, I hope it provides a productive theoretical scaffolding that can be applied, adapted, and revised in relation to such stories.

I also focus on "race" and racism to the exclusion of other social oppressions, which I mention only in passing. This is largely because black feminist critiques figure prominently in the literature—perhaps because racial politics have been so prominent in the United States, where many of the activists and theorists I draw upon have been based. It is also because doing justice to any singular body of work is difficult enough; I am unlikely to do justice to the rich discussions now percolating around settler colonialism and sexualities in particular within a relatively short book.

To help the reader appreciate where the ideas I discuss emerge from, I provide some broad historical and textual context. The first chapter is the most "historical" as I set the context for why work matters to feminists at all. I do so by tracing the ways in which capitalism's emergence altered the meaning of work within people's lives. In the following chapters, I include briefer, usually introductory, passages that describe socio-political trends in the development of capitalism relevant to those writing about women's work at the time. I hope readers wanting more extended discussions of the feminists and issues I touch upon briefly will find the endnotes helpful.

Women and Work: Feminism, Labour, and Social Reproduction is a book about theory. But it is about theory that is needed if we are to create a world which prioritizes meeting human needs for security, health, sustenance, and creativity before all else. If the demonstrations and women's strikes of recent years are to develop into a truly mass, pluralist, anti-capitalist movement, socialists and socialist feminists need to sort through the competing ideas that guide their political decision making. We need to work through to a more theoretically coherent perspective, one that can make a clear and compelling case for placing the fight against oppression at the heart of the class struggle. I hope this book contributes to that project.

1

The Labour Lens

Why do feminists think about work at all? What makes work—or labour—a compelling lens through which to view the world? I can think of a few good answers to that question. The most obvious perhaps is that the vast majority of women today work, and they work a lot, often under difficult and degrading circumstances. To begin, women do the majority—75 percent—of the world's unpaid care and domestic work. They spend up to three hours more per day cooking and cleaning than men do, and anywhere from two to ten hours more per day looking after children and the elderly.[1] Whatever the hardship or rewards of such work, it remains the case that those who govern our countries and economies do not recompense or adequately recognize it as a contribution to overall social wealth. As for paid labour, women's global participation rates are lower than men's, but after 300-plus years of capitalism, women are still more likely to land in the informal and low-waged sectors. They are still more likely to earn their living doing jobs that are arduous, dangerous, and insecure.[2]

That these patterns prevail makes it not just reasonable, but in fact urgent, to ask what women's work has to do with gender and gender oppression.[3] Feminists began seriously engaging with that question at the dawn of industrial capitalism. That we return to it today is not so much a sign of their failure to find an answer as it is of society's failure to solve the problem of work, and of women's work in particular. This book is about the responses to that question. It stretches back to the earliest Western feminist tracts and leapfrogs the centuries to consider feminist ideas about labour today. It is not, however, a mere review of what wise women (and some men) have had to say. Rather, it reflects upon the ways in which those ideas developed in order, primarily, to understand why the socialist feminist tradition has struggled to articulate a coherent, inclusive anti-oppression politics, and how the renewal of social reproduction feminism can most effectively contribute to anti-capitalist projects today. I introduce the book's argument and structure below.

But this chapter begins with a consideration of what work is, and why it matters so much for those who want to change the world.

CAPITALISM, WORK, AND WOMEN

There's a reason that Euro-Western feminists started thinking and writing about work when they did. It has to do with capitalism. The emergence of capitalist social relations in sixteenth- and seventeenth-century England, and their imposition and consolidation throughout the United Kingdom, the continent, and the colonies over the next 150 years was founded on a dramatic and violent reorganization of people's working lives. The nature of the work people did, the times of day they performed it, who they worked with and for, and *why* they worked changed radically. Once a means of *supporting* life, work became a means even of *dominating* life as well.

Feudal peasants and serfs did indeed spend their lives working—often under harsh conditions. But work was something they did to survive. They did not also, as those who live in capitalist societies must, *survive to work*. Unlike waged workers, peasants and serfs had direct access to the wider ecosystem on which their subsistence depended. They produced the food they ate and chopped the wood they used for warmth and shelter. And they exercised significant control over the rhythms and pace of daily and seasonal tasks, and over the uses of communal lands and water. Their work satisfied specific, pre-determined needs (needs that exceeded bare subsistence to include spirituality, ritual, and play).[4]

Marx refers to this relation of the peasantry to the land as "the natural unity of labour with its material [*sachlich*] presuppositions."[5] This pre-capitalist mode of existence is premised upon a birth-given (and therefore seemingly natural) position within the wider social order. While that position is dependent upon and subordinate to the direct, personal authority of a lord, belonging to a lord in feudal Europe went hand-in-hand with belonging to the land. Whatever hardship lords inflicted, the peasantry was already, by custom and law, attached to the land from which its members could (however meagerly) feed, clothe, and shelter themselves.[6] Given their direct access to the means of subsistence, the peasantry can sustain itself outside of the peasant-lord relation. The peasant has "an objective existence independent of labour," writes Marx, similar to a "proprietor," who can shape "the conditions of his reality." But unlike the *nonproductive* proprietor (a lord or capitalist for instance), the peasantry is a community of "co-proprietors ... who at the same time work."[7]

This is not to say the peasantry exercised total control over its working conditions. Lords and estate managers decided what got produced on feudal estates, when and how. Moreover, those decisions, and to a certain extent those of peasant households as well, were set according to patriarchal conventions that enforced a traditional (if not absolute) gender division of labour, granting women only precarious and partial control over their bodies and labour. But access to the means of subsistence granted peasants and serfs considerable ability to set the rhythms and pace of their labours. They ceased work for festivals and holidays and, if pushed to intensify production or pay higher taxes, they regularly extended midday breaks or left crops in the fields to rot.[8] Lords responded by exacting penalties and more closely supervising peasant labour. But they could not kick the peasantry off the land, effectively threatening recalcitrant producers with starvation. Though politically subordinate, peasants and serfs were under no *economic* compulsion to obey the lords.

All this changes—over time, and with tremendous struggle—with the rise of capitalism. Capitalist social relations emerge first in the English countryside in the sixteenth and seventeenth centuries and become the dominant mode of production in rural and urban areas across the continent over the next 150 years. The uneven, violent, and ongoing transition from feudalism to capitalism need not be recounted here in detail.[9] At its heart is the expropriation of the peasantry—the razing of household plots and enclosures of common lands that, in time, sever the direct relationship of the peasant to her own means of subsistence. For Marx, this process generates the "primitive accumulation of capital": it transforms "individualized and scattered means of production into socially concentrated means of production" essential to kickstart (and sustain) capitalism.[10]

No longer are decisions about what gets produced in the hands of lords and peasants. With the rise of capitalism, the *market* (that is, the competitive dynamic among capitalists and independent producers) determines production. Labour, then, becomes something more than a practical human activity to be set in motion to meet specific needs and desires. It becomes a means of producing commodities: things that the market determines hold economic value—things that will produce a profit. Whereas in feudal society, the needs and desires of the aristocracy were excessive, they were not endless. Capitalist production, however, has no such inherent limit. Unlike the peasant who exercised some control over how quickly and when she hoed fields for the lord, baked bread for her household, and broke from her labours to eat, drink, and sleep, the waged worker is forced to adopt new forms of work discipline.[11] This ensures that one-time "co-proprietors ... who also work" learn precisely what it means to be (property-less) workers ... who also live.

The work of living, of sustaining oneself when not working for the capitalist, does not disappear of course. It just goes underground. It becomes separated from and subsumed to the work of *making a living*—earning a wage in order to buy what is necessary to create and maintain life. The marginalization of unwaged subsistence work does not occur because waged work is harder or more important. It occurs because the work of subsisting, of reproducing life, is no longer possible unless one, *first*, has access to a wage (or other forms of money income). Some people avoid waged work by selling or trading things they make. But most, unable to feed and shelter themselves by directly and productively appropriating the means of life from the forests, fields, and waters, end up working for a wage—a wage with which they buy food, shelter, and clothing. In this way, work for a capitalist comes to dominate *all* "life-activity"—not just the value-producing activity of the factory floor or other workplace.

As in feudalism, then, most people in capitalist societies certainly work to survive. *But they also survive to work.* More precisely, they survive to become waged labourers. But here's the crux: to become waged labourers is itself a feat of labour—of women's labour specifically. While women's work varied across region and time in feudal peasant societies, women performed the bulk of the tasks required to meet subsistence needs.[12] They cooked, cleaned, and looked after young children. They also tilled the soil and harvested the produce of fields and garden plots, butchered animals, brewed beer, spun yarn, and ground grains. They developed and administered medicines to heal the sick. And they attended other women in labour, gave birth, and nursed new life. In short, women—in a more direct and transparent way than men—reproduced human beings.

With the transition to capitalism, women's reproductive labour is radically reorganized. First, as peasants lose their access to land, women lose direct access to and control over the "material presuppositions" of their subsistence-based activities. Men of course lose this too, but women's reproductive work *remains* outside the immediate value circuits of capitalism (even as the product of that work, human beings, move in and out of those circuits as present and future waged workers, and even as women are themselves drawn into waged work on a massive scale). What's more, women's subsistence work is, in this early stage of capitalist development, increasingly distinguished from waged work spatially and temporally. It is generally performed in communities and private households (away from work performed for capitalists) and at times that accommodate the waged workers' workday, week, and year.

Responsible for reproducing workers, women in capitalist societies are at the heart of an intractable dilemma. Capitalist profit-making—and, thus, the existence of capitalism itself—depends upon the availability of the very human labour power whose means of subsistence it has already appropriated. It becomes imperative to regulate women's labour, especially if, as was often the case, there are not enough workers willing and able to submit to the new capitalist disciplines of work. Capitalist states and ruling classes partially resolve this dilemma by turning women's bodies "into an instrument for the reproduction of labor and the expansion of the work-force."[13] Thus, as Maria Mies and Silvia Federici contend, the primitive accumulation of capital involves more than the expropriation of European workers' land (and the enslavement of African bodies). It also, crucially, requires the expropriation of women's reproductive labour.

Yet *that* was not going to happen without a struggle. Without doubt, feudal society was deeply patriarchal. Women were, for the most part, legally subject to the authority wielded by fathers, husbands, curates, and lords. Still, within peasant households and communities, inequality was tempered, on the one hand, by the control women exercised over their (re)productive labours and, on the other, by the fact that *both* men and women were subject to a higher patriarchal authority, the lord. Capitalism's consolidation then required the gradual, uneven, and ongoing, frequently violent, process of undermining the control and relative equality women enjoyed in peasant households. A burgeoning capitalist state (supported by the Catholic Church and male-dominated craft guilds) variously terrorized, compelled, and induced women to accept new forms of sexist degradation and domesticity. Poor women faced persecution as witches and saw their work as midwives and healers sidelined, diminishing women's control over abortion, live births, and contraception. The state also intensified women's social vulnerability, introducing changes to inheritance laws, criminalizing prostitution, legalizing rape and battery, and ousting women from certain forms of paid labour.

"Throughout the 16th and 17th centuries," observes Federici, "women lost ground in every area of social life."[14]

In time, marriage and motherhood (when they were not outrightly forced on women) appeared a reasonable, perhaps the only sensible, option. Many women resisted their disempowerment and fought for control over their own fertility. Nonetheless, modern gender relations (characterized by the separation of a public sphere of industry and politics from the private domestic sphere, and women's relative isolation within and primary responsibility for the latter) eventually prevailed.[15] "Housewification," as Mies calls it, takes hold first within bourgeois households, which could absorb the loss of the wife's income from paid labour or professions. Only later, in the mid- to late nineteenth century, after the introduction of protective legislation and a period of wages climbing relative to the cost of living, do increasing numbers of married working class women become full-time housewives.

WORK, LIFE, HISTORY

Capitalism thus radically disrupts people's relationship to work and life—a fact Marx spent his life explaining. And while he subjects capitalist forms of work to a brilliant and excoriating critique, his analysis rests on a broader, transhistorical, claim that labour is a precondition of all human life. Grasping what he means by this lends some insight into women's unique relationship to work, to life, and to capital.[16]

Marx arrives at his insight about work and life by pondering how people are positioned in relation to nature. It is not an idle question. Like all social theorists, he aims to understand the dynamics of human society. Society would not be possible, he reasons, without human interaction with the natural world. Rather than conceiving of society and nature as two distinct or opposing realities, however, he begins his analysis by stressing their coherence or identity. That is, the events, processes, and institutions created to serve human ends are produced out of—and are therefore an integral part of—the nonhuman, physical world constituted by plants, animals, land, water, and climate.

Not only is the social world *part of* the wider natural world with which humans also interact, according to Marx, but humans themselves are *of* that world. Humans *are* nature. In his notebooks on economics and philosophy, he observes: "Man *lives* on nature—means that nature is his *body*, with which he must remain in continuous interchange if he is not to die. That man's physical and spiritual life is linked to nature means simply that nature is linked to itself, for man is a part of nature."[17]

This leads Marx to propose that human existence and the reproduction of human life depend upon a person's ability to "appropriate the materials of nature in a form adapted to his own needs."[18] Somewhat confusingly, the term "appropriate" in this passage does not signal the act of simply taking or owning something (as it does when Marx refers to capitalist appropriation). Instead, it means *production*—"practical human activity" or *work* in the broadest sense.[19] Unless people *productively appropriate* from the oceans, lakes, fields, and forests to create food, shelter, clothes, and more, there can be no human life. Yet in so doing, Marx observes, humans and their society are (*must be*) also distinct from nature. They are, therefore, both part of nature *and* external to it.[20]

Unlike most nonhuman animals, people engage in productive appropriation *consciously*.[21] They interact with nature not simply out of instinct, but with awareness of their needs and the ability and intent to design specific ways of meeting those needs. This is what separates, Marx famously writes, the weaver from the spider, the architect from the bee: the capacity to bring *ideas* and *imagination* to bear on the bio-physical interaction with nature required for human survival. *This* is the essence of human labour or work in general.

As the inescapable precondition for human life, work is a timeless, existential reality—"the eternal natural necessity of human life ... independent of any particular form of this life."[22] Yet precisely because work is a conscious, practical activity, it is also the precondition and the substance of human *history*. To suggest that work (or labour or production) is historical is simply to suggest that it is shaped by and is part of shaping the social world (as opposed to being determined by natural or divine forces, for example). Specifically, work sets in motion an open-ended, ever-changing dialectic between human subjects and the conditions shaping their broader world: "Man acts upon external nature and changes it, and in this way he simultaneously changes his own nature. He develops the potentialities slumbering within nature, and subjects the play of its forces to his own sovereign power."[23]

The suggestion that "man subjects the play of [nature's] forces to his own sovereign power" jumps off the page today—evidence, it would seem, that Marx urges the domination of nature to human ends, whatever the cost. That, however, is a gross misreading of his work. Marx posits a *metabolic* relationship between humans and nature: as natural, *embodied* beings, humans exist inside a wider ecosystem, and thus their survival depends upon the survival of the entire system. As Marx well knows despite the imagery he invokes, humans do not truly exercise "sovereign power." They are not—cannot be—endlessly, relentlessly, recklessly productive. Rather, their creative powers constantly bump up against the limits of that wider system. For instance, the fertility of the soil, the abundance of minerals in the ground, the number of available producers, or the vagaries of climate are all natural, exhaustible features of the world that set real limits to production.[24]

The determining conditions of what does and does not get produced, and how the production and reproduction of life and the world are organized, however, are not simply natural. They are also social. When Marx writes, "Men make their own history, but they do not make it as they please; they do not make it under self-selected circumstances, but under circumstances existing already, given and transmitted from the past," he is referring to the social relations of dependence and autonomy, of domination and freedom, that adhere among people.[25] For these social relations also comprise the wider ecosystem. And they also, *crucially*, shape the possibilities of how, as Mies puts it, "human beings *produce their lives*."[26]

This is the grounding insight of historical materialism: human labour or work—the practical, conscious interaction between people and the natural world of which they are part—creates the social processes and relations that, in turn, determine the processes and relations of that labour. Our understanding of those relations cannot proceed then without understanding work, just as our understanding of work cannot proceed without understanding the social world. "Work" in this reckoning is expansive. It includes the things people do to create their entire worlds—not just their labour for lords or capitalists. Hoeing fields, assembling cars, and mining coal are certainly part of that work. But so are tasks such as wiping runny noses, clearing dishes from the table, writing poetry, and organizing birding expeditions. As we'll see in the coming chapters, it is precisely this expansiveness that captures feminist imaginations—both as a lever of social critique and as a vision for building alternative worlds.

None of this means that work is an inherently good or bad activity (although it does mean it has a definite value to human life). Neither does it mean that there are no other conceptual windows through which one can gain insight into how the world works. It simply establishes that work is an existential reality of our lives and our worlds. It is "life-activity."[27] And because it is shaped in and through people's relationships with each other, work changes in accordance with changes in those relationships—relationships that are characterized by more or less freedom and equality. Work is thus also a premise of human history. Its social form—how work is organized—matters to how freely, or not, people create their worlds, their societies, their lives. Inquiring into the social organization of work, then, is essential if social theory is to serve freedom. And that is precisely why feminists grapple with the question of work. And it is why theories of labour attentive to the dynamics of gender offer valuable insight into understanding the forces of oppression and freedom.

WOMEN'S WORK AND FEMINIST THEORY

Over the course of the eighteenth century, the places, times, and rhythms of women's work changed remarkably. Not only did women lose considerable control over the conditions of their unpaid reproductive labour, their paid labour also changed. Women were swept out of certain occupations only to be swept into others as cheap, expendable labourers. In the process, the conventional gender division of labour took on new meanings. Women's reproductive work in capitalist societies remained essential, and therefore something still to be managed and controlled. But the forms and mechanisms of that control shift. Most pointedly, such work was radically separated from direct production for capitalists and thereby devalued.

It is not surprising then that as capitalist relations in the United Kingdom and Europe consolidated, feminists began to examine women's work, considering its significance to questions of freedom and oppression. Their views challenged contemporary thinking about work by affirming the social value of women's domestic responsibilities and women's competence to participate in occupations from which they had been excluded. In time, they also insisted that household activities constitute *work* (as opposed to a divinely ordained duty). The significance of this last point bears emphasizing. In identifying caring for the home and family as work, feminists defied the dominant capitalist understanding of labour as something done for a wage—that is, as a directly value-generating, market-based activity. They defied, that is, the perception of labour that informs so much political economy from Adam Smith and on. In so doing, they launched a discussion about work's fuller, fleshier contours, a discussion still carried on today—one that begins not from abstract concepts of value but from concrete observations of work's embodied and gendered realities.

Late eighteenth- and early nineteenth-century feminists thereby planted the seeds of a radical revisioning of what constitutes labour. This book traces that revisioning as it develops along three trajectories: (i) equality feminism, (ii) critical equality feminism, and (iii) social reproduction feminism. Each trajectory troubles the capitalist organization of the gender division of labour. And each sees women's work—and women's unpaid reproductive work in particular—as significant to women's oppression. But their understanding of its significance varies. The coming chapters explore these distinct, albeit interrelated, lines of thinking about work. Beginning with the pre-capitalist European tracts known as the *querelle des femmes*, and moving through the centuries, I distill from the massive body of feminist literature those texts that best articulate the advance in the equality, critical equality, and social reproduction feminism perspectives.

Whatever their differences, these perspectives share a common impulse to attend to the gendered dynamics of work. They also share a fatal oversight: the tendency to ignore work's racial dynamics. This begins with failing to see the *racialized* underbelly that attended "housewification" and the devaluation of women's waged work. For, as Mies, Federici, and others have shown, the modern European "housewife" is not simply a product of patriarchal capitalism. She is the product of a racist, colonial patriarchal capitalism. She is the product, that is, of the plundering of faraway lands, bodies, and other labouring peoples, whose subjection is justified through bogus, racist scientific and religious discourse about a white civilizing mission.

To begin, insofar as her demure sexuality and release from paid labour marks her as "civilized" (and therefore distinct from colonized, brown-skinned, "savages"), the white European housewife is part and parcel of the colonial project's racist ideological wrappings. She is literally and figuratively the creation of man's domination of sensual, gritty, uncontrolled nature.[28] Moreover, to some extent, the working class housewife's release from paid labour is bound up with the exploitation of colonial lands and people. In the mid-nineteenth century, the degradation and dehumanization of workers and slaves on colonial estates in India, Africa, Indonesia, and the Americas kept the price of sugar, coffee, tea, cotton, and other staples low. At the same time, the British state passed protective legislation barring women from certain forms of paid employment. Major trade unions, workingmen's associations, and pundits supported the move (which was accompanied by a slight increase in men's wages as compensation), arguing that women's place was in the home.[29] The coincidence of protective legislation and a lower cost of living allowed Western workers to stretch their wages further than before, arguably making housewification possible for many—though certainly not all—working class women by the late 1800s.

Thus, women's household work at the time feminists began to critically examine it is grounded not just in an unequal and oppressive gender division of labour, but in racist, colonial enterprises as well—a fact white, Euro-feminists generally failed to note. Some criticized slavery and supported the abolition movement, but beyond commenting on parallels between the social treatment of women and enslaved people, early white feminists simply did not attempt to think through how racism also shapes women's work. And even though African American abolitionists began drawing attention to this in the nineteenth century, inaugurating a tradition of anti-racist feminist thought that repeatedly insisted on the integrated nature of social oppressions, later white feminists across the three trajectories barely engaged with their ideas. In part, as I argue in Chapter 6, this has to do with white feminist thinking about labour focusing too narrowly on the very theoretical innovation for which it is most known: attributing positive social and economic value to women's unpaid work in the home. How and why this innovation proves so troublesome becomes clear as we track its development through the centuries of feminist thinking about work.

PART I

THREE TRAJECTORIES

2

The Rational-Humanist Roots
of Equality Feminism

The earliest feminists paid little heed to the upheaval in women's working lives described in the last chapter.[1] They had other dragons to slay. Most notably, they were preoccupied with responding to the "onslaught of vilification and contempt" directed at women from the fifteenth century onward by spokesmen for a nascent merchant-bourgeois order.[2] Anxious to spoof and degrade the chivalric values of the aristocracy they hoped to replace, members of this male cultural elite wrote plays, poems, and fables inveighing against women, love, and marriage. These, alongside medieval clerical misogynist tracts, inspired a 25-year-old widow of a French royal secretary, Christine de Pizan, to respond. Christine's polemic, *Le livre de la cité des dames* (1405), inaugurated the so-called *querelle des femmes*—which Joan Kelly describes as a four-century-long literary debate "about women and sexual politics in European society before the French Revolution."[3]

Contributors to this debate did not, in most cases, directly or substantially address the issue of women's work. They focused instead on establishing women's moral and intellectual equality with men, framing women's oppression in terms of the absence or presence of reason. Yet, as capitalist gender relations consolidated—that is, as the radical separation of the public and private spheres became entrenched and a middle class cult of domesticity spread—feminists began to discuss women's work more directly and consistently. The second half of this chapter reveals how late eighteenth-century radical democratic feminists set the stage for the *equality feminist* theorization of labour.

My reading of this period responds to Barbara Taylor's influential argument about radical democratic feminist Mary Wollstonecraft. Taylor contends that Wollstonecraft's egalitarianism anticipates the innovations of utopian socialist feminism.[4] This claim, however, obscures an important development in feminist thinking about women's work. As I argue in Chapter 3, utopian socialist feminism evolves out of a political-economic critique of unpaid domestic work. Wollstone-craft, though disparaging of gross inequalities of wealth, grounds her feminism within the same moral philosophical traditions advanced within the *querelle*. In extending a rational-humanist critique that cele-brates women as equal, autonomous human beings, she and other radical democratic feminists position work (and a positive work ethic) as a key means of ending women's oppression.

"JUST AS CLEVER AS THE MALE SEX": THE *QUERELLE* AND INEQUALITY

In *Cité des dames*, Christine de Pizan challenges the received wisdom of medieval France that judges women as irrational, morally depraved, and intellectually unfit for civic life. She appeals to Lady Reason, Lady Rectitude, and Lady Justice to mount an empirical argument about women's equality with men. Her goal is to prove the folly and injustice of the philosophers, satirists, orators, and others who "have said and continue to say and write such awful, damning things about women and their ways."[5]

If women appear to be of lesser competence and virtue than men, it is not due to any natural or divine plan. It is because they have not had the chance to prove themselves. They are held back, she writes in passing, specifically because women "are less exposed to a wide variety of expe-riences and activities for expanding the mind since they have to stay at home all day to look after the household."[6] Yet history's great women are evidence that "the female sex is just as clever as the male sex."[7] Their apparent inferiority is thus a *cultural* construction, reflective of the misogyny borne of men's "fears, interests and concerns."[8] Allow reason to prevail, and inequality will wither away.

Christine rests her case for men's and women's shared humanity on empirical evidence and reason. A similar embrace of rational-humanist principles runs through the hundreds of tracts defending women published over the next 400 years. Like Christine, early European feminists marshal evidence from history, scripture, and their own expe-riences to insist that women are men's equals in spirit and mind, if not necessarily in body—although they regularly highlight women's strength, knowledge, and leadership in past military campaigns. They "stood for a truly general conception of humanity," one that embraces an ideal of woman (and men) as educated, independent, and free from tyranny.[9]

Although many mention women's responsibility for the household and restricted access to occupations, they offer little substantial or sustained analysis of women's work.

The English contributions to the *querelle* are of special interest here as they coincide with the immense social and cultural upheaval associated with the rise of capitalism. While French feudalism survived for 300 years after the publication of *Cité des dames*, the English landed gentry drove the expansion and intensification of capitalist social relations in the countryside, chipping away at feudal relations with considerable violence. As early as the sixteenth century, capitalism emerged in England as the new form of social domination. Thus, the 400 years of the *querelle* are the same 400 years of British capital's unabated struggle to consolidate rule through colonial conquest and slavery, dispossession and enclosures, internationalization of trade, the deepening and extending of agrarian and manufacturing industries, and—crucially for our purposes—a realignment of gender relations.

British state, church and civil society all contributed to this realignment. Fifteenth- and sixteenth-century measures outlawing begging, prostitution, witchcraft, and certain religious sects "strengthened the household as an instrument of social control ... herded people into households for their livelihood and placed unpropertied males—and all women—under the governance of the household 'master.'"[10] Whereas women labourers, tenants, and entrepreneurs at the end of the fourteenth century appear to have represented themselves at manorial courts in debt and property disputes, and many lived with men without first marrying them, new laws and the canonical courts began to restrict their (relative) independence. In urban centers, medieval borough customs allowing wives to trade slowly disappeared, such that by the nineteenth century, only married women in London could expect to engage in trade.[11] Lacking a legal identity distinct from their husbands, women had few options for survival if their marriages soured.

British spinsters and widows enjoyed more economic rights than married women over this period. In sixteenth- and seventeenth-century Oxford, for example, they owned property and ran taverns, glove- and shoe-making operations and were often shopkeepers too. But they were excluded from participating in guilds regulating their businesses and had restricted access to apprentices. Meanwhile, no laws prevented married or single working class women from toiling in fields, mines, middle class homes, and factories, where they earned one-third to one-half of men doing similar jobs. By the early nineteenth century, about two-thirds of married working class women worked for a wage.[12] As capitalist relations matured, then, most women took part in some form of paid labour outside of the household. While pressures to confine women to the private, patriarchal household intensified, only a small layer of better off women were in a position to do so.

Pressures to keep women "in their place" were especially forceful during the English Civil Wars, as male polemicists responded to the audaciousness of those who dared defy patriarchal conventions. By the 1640s, women were a fixture in the groundswell of sectarian opposition to Church and King. Brownists, Lollards, Quakers, and other radical freethinkers preaching spiritual equality between the sexes had been attracting laywomen to their churches for decades. Women not only took the pulpit, they also vied for roles in church government, defying St. Paul's prohibition in the Book of Corinthians. Some sects put into practice Diggers leader Gerrard Winstanley's ideal society in which "every man and woman shall have the free liberty to marry whom they love."[13] No doubt shocking to the "respectable" classes, such practices were not new. Preaching sexual freedom, writes Christopher Hill, "gave ideological form and coherent expression to practices which had long been common among vagabonds, squatter-cottagers, and the in-between category of migratory craftsmen."[14]

All this emboldened some women to push for more. Mary Tattle-well and Joane Hit-him-home mounted an especially militant and explicit challenge to patriarchal culture in their 1640 screed, *The Womens* (*sic.*) *Sharpe Revenge*. The self-proclaimed spinster authors turn the tables on male polemicists, accusing men of being "inconstant … voracious and insatiate."[15] Women, they aver, are not just equal to men but are *more fit* to run businesses and the country. Their opponents responded in kind, castigating women preachers as "hussys" and "disobedient." In the next breath, however, they deemed women frail and incompetent, "apt to be seduced, strong in their affections, and loving too much Independency, but weak and easy in their understandings, not able to examine grounds and reasons, nor to answer you."[16] Women's offence was not knowing their place, to "have rather been a husband than a wife … and a magistrate than a subject."[17]

While attacks on women's supposed wanton sexuality, loose morals, and inferior minds did not disappear—they were, in fact, prominent in crushing the 1649 radicals—a more protective, apparently pro-women inflection crept into Restoration-era discourse. In sermons and articles, men admired women for their submissiveness and virtuousness, their rhetoric aimed at inducing rather than haranguing women to accept their domestic calling within male-headed households.

Feminists were not persuaded. In *Some Reflections upon Marriage* (1700) Mary Astell writes, "if absolute Sovereignty be not necessary in a State, how comes it to be so in a Family? … why is Slavery so much condemn'd and strove against in one Case, and so highly applauded, and held so necessary and so sacred in another."[18] Such comparisons of marriage and slavery are a recurring feminist theme—not because both housewives and the enslaved are not paid for their labour but because each system denies a person's full humanity. Insofar as marriage binds women legally to their husbands, society fails to recognize them (like the enslaved) as persons of equal moral worth and ability. Moral *dependence*—not *labour*—is the key axis of critique with *querelle* feminism, signaling the (irrational) legal, canonical, and cultural restrictions binding women to men.

If men's arbitrary authority was the problem, then advocating for women's education seemed an appropriate response. Astell urges women's education as a means of avoiding marriage (educated women are better equipped to live collectively, free of men's interference). More commonly, however, feminists agreed with Bathsua Pell Makin that educated women make better wives and mothers, as well as being "very useful to their Husbands in their Trades." The idea of educating oneself for professional advancement, she adds, is useful only for spinsters and widows who must "understand and manage their own affairs."[19]

Decades later, the link between education and economic independence is made with greater force and frequency. The Sophia tracts, published in 1739 and 1740, make the case, advocating women's access to medical, legal, and military training, while an anonymous contributor to the *Gentleman's Magazine* "challenged the usurpation of female occupations by men, and predicted that the continuing lack of occupations for women would become even more of a pressing issue."[20] To be sure, these and other arguments were mostly made by, on behalf of, and to elite women—hence the overwhelming focus on women's access to *occupations* and the scant attention paid to industrial jobs, fieldwork, and domestic service. This naturalization of class differences and tendency to limit the feminist ideal of independence to women in the upper ranks of society runs throughout the *querelle*. Labouring women are sometimes present in the shadows—in references, for example, to women's respon-sibilities for managing their household staff. Or they are the objects of pity and philanthropy, their *poverty* considered a problem, but not the jobs they do.

Sarah Robinson Scott's life and work typifies such an approach. Scott paid for twelve poor women to attend charity schools, but her popular 1762 novel suggests she had no illusions that schooling would (or should) level class distinctions. *Millenium* (*sic.*) *Hall* is a tale of five wealthy women who run a school for women. While the women hold property in common, the school itself is open only to uplift "indigent gentle-women" who have been "reduced" to a state of dependence.[21] Working class children are trained elsewhere for menial work, and their sisters and mothers offered jobs in a carpet factory. Advocating for expanded opportunities in education and work was not uncommon among *querelle* feminists, but not at the risk of disrupting class relations.

Texts penned by two of the handful of working class women to con-tribute to the *querelle* stand out for their more expansive understanding of work. The poetry of washerwoman Mary Collier is the first and most substantive tract to "defend laboring women as laboring women."[22] Responding directly to a poem ridiculing and trivializing women field-workers, *The Woman's Labour* (1739) describes women hoeing, planting, and harvesting, as well as cooking and cleaning in the homes of the rich. *And* it chronicles the work women do to feed, clean, and care for members of their own households—contrasting the boundlessness and seamless-ness of women's work to men's shorter and more defined workday:

> … WHEN Ev'ning does approach, we homeward hi
> And our domestick Toils incessant ply:
> Against your coming Home prepare to get
> Our Work all don, Our House in order set;
> Bacon and Dumpling in the Pots we boil,
> Our Beds we make, our Swine we feed the while;
> And set the Table out against you come:
> Early next Morning owe on you attend,
> Our tender Babes unto the Field we bear
> And wrap them in our Cloaths to keep them warm,
> While round about we gather up the Corn;[23]

While other *querelle* feminists may have pitied or extolled poor women for their hard work, they rarely discussed the actual waged and unwaged labour most women perform—and they never connected it to the issue of gender inequality. Collier's poem calls on readers to do just that: recognize the dignity and value of the full gambit of women's work while also pointing out the inequality between men's and women's work lives.

If few addressed working class women's lot, even fewer addressed the experiences of the enslaved women whose labour enriched imperial Britain. Mary Ferguson singles out Aphra Behn's 1698 novella, *Oroonoko, or The Royal Slave*, about an enslaved West African prince and his lover as "an amazing exception to the near absence of protest against slavery" at the time.[24] But Behn's book says little about slave *labour*. And her critique, like that of later feminist abolitionists, focuses on the injustice and irrationality of denying universal freedom and humanity to a portion of the human race, while only ambiguously condemning slavery as a system of labour.[25]

One intriguing, though fleeting, exception to this treatment of slavery is found in the poetry of Ann Cromartie Yearsley—another working class contributor to the *querelle*. In *A Poem on the Inhumanity of the Slave-Trade* (1788), Yearsley glimpses a connection between the wealth of the nation and the source of that wealth in slave labour. She writes of England's "Commerce" draining "a fellow-creature's blood," and then continues:

> ... Must our wants
> Find their supply in murder? Shall the sons
> Of Commerce shif'ting stand, if not employ'd
> Worse than the midnight robber?[26]

Yearsley and Collier both offer flashes of new perspectives on labour. Most early feminists conceptualized work in two related ways: as a positive moral imperative that signaled a person's humanity, and as a potential path to independence from, and thus equality with, men. Women's inequality, in this view, stems primarily from obstacles society puts in the way to fulfilling their potential as autonomous human beings—from legal and cultural forces denying women higher education and confining them to the household. Such obstacles are attributed to the circulation of irrational, outdated ideas and practices. They do not arise from the forms and differential values of work itself.

By contrast, Yearsley and Collier suggest that the social form and value of work matter. While dissecting the daily, concrete tasks of working class women, Collier roots inequality in the gender division of labour, alluding to the idea that women's household work is undervalued and invisible—anticipating a theme that comes to dominate later feminist critiques of women's work. Yearsley's innovation is less specifically about women's work. Its significance lies in its affinity with a vein of radical democratic political economy that identifies labour as productive of economic value.[27] In questioning the justice of extracting value from unpaid (slave) labour, Yearsley shifts, albeit briefly, away from the rational-humanism that characterizes *querelle* feminism, gesturing toward a political economic analysis that utopian socialists later elaborate.

Collier and Yearsley, however, are exceptions. *Querelle* feminists overwhelmingly drew on rational-humanist premises to critique women's place in society. The feminists to close out the eighteenth century did not veer from that approach—even as they innovated by more directly assessing the issue of women's work, positioning labour as a specifically feminist issue.

WOLLSTONECRAFT AND EQUALITY FEMINISM

Just as the English Civil Wars fired up the polemical forces for and against women's equality, so too did the French Revolution. In October 1789, the "market-women" of Paris organized a march on Versailles to protest the price and scarcity of bread. Like the storming of the Bastille, this thousands-strong armed act of resistance was a defining moment of the revolution.[28] It led to the formation of revolutionary clubs in which women asserted their political rights, inspiring playwright Olympe de Gouges to pen her *Déclaration des droits de la femme et de la citoyenne* in 1791. Among other rights, she demanded that women "be equally entitled to all public honours, positions and employment according to their capacities and with no other distinctions than those based solely on talent and virtue."[29]

Although the Reign of Terror soon put an end to feminist activism in France (Olympe de Gouges was one of many feminist rebels executed in 1793), women across the channel took up the torch. They were greeted with much hostility and derision. In the words of one offended detractor, "*unsexed* female writers ... now instruct, or confuse, us and themselves in the labyrinth of politicks, or turn us wild with Gallick frenzy."[30] The best known and most influential target of such attacks was Mary Wollstonecraft, whose *A Vindication of the Rights of Woman* appeared in 1792.

Three broad influences shape Wollstonecraft's feminism: a radical democratic commitment to social equality, a powerful belief in the social construction of character, and a religious utopianism that insists upon the perfectibility of humankind. While her egalitarianism sets Wollstonecraft apart from more conservative *querelle* feminists, her ideas are continuous with that tradition in other important ways.[31] The central plea in *Vindication*—to bring about "a revolution in female manners" necessary for women to stand equally with men—is consistent with the long-standing focus on reshaping women's character to more competently act in a man's world.[32] Also like her predecessors, Wollstonecraft argues that such a revolution requires a general shift away from the hegemony of arbitrary power. Unless kings and nobles can "throw off their gaudy hereditary trappings," she claims, women are bound to seek power in similarly irrational ways.[33] That is, they will rely on the (irrational) power of beauty rather than their minds.

These ideas are grounded solidly in the conviction that women are, like men, potentially autonomous, free and rational beings limited by the irrational world they inhabit. "The woman of wisdom and virtue ... is one who can 'forget her sex even at that time of life when sexual consciousness is most insistent, promoting in herself instead those capacities common to all humanity, 'regardless of the distinction of sex.'"[34] As many before her had done, she counsels women to sharpen their rational faculties through higher levels of classical schooling. Equal education with men equips them to better fulfill their natural, God-given destiny— which is to be "properly attentive to their domestic duties."[35] Education also allows women to prove their mettle as physicians, nurses, midwives, or managers of a shop or farm.

This is familiar territory. Yet Wollstonecraft stands out for the degree to which, more consistently and systematically than many of her predecessors, she also advances a forceful critique of inequality in general. Education alone, she insists, cannot undo the damage of a society based on inherited wealth and arbitrary government. Women will never be men's equals so long as the corrupting influence of aristocratic rule *and wealth* persists. Rather, they will simply adopt the same irrational power ploys they see playing out among feeble-minded aristocrats:

When men neglect the duties of humanity, women will follow their example; a common stream hurries them both along with thoughtless celerity. Riches and honours prevent a man from enlarging his understanding, and enervate all his powers by reversing the order of nature, which has ever made true pleasure the reward of labour. Pleasure— enervating pleasure is, likewise, within women's reach without earning it. But, till hereditary possessions are spread abroad, how can we expect men to be proud of virtue? And, till they are, women will govern them by the most direct means, neglecting their dull domestic duties to catch the pleasure that is on the wing of time.[36]

Wollstonecraft attacks not just aristocratic privilege but specifically condemns excessive wealth. This leads Taylor to trumpet her "uncompromising egalitarianism"—a commitment which links Wollstonecraft's view of women's emancipation to the "elimination of *all* hierarchical divisions … of rank, sex, age, race, and wealth." Wollstonecraft, she explains, was part of "a small band of ultra-radical intellectuals" with a millenarian conviction that a utopia of equals was possible on earth—a conviction that her critics associated with the radical views of the English Civil War sect, the Levellers.[37] Taylor traces this radical critique to Wollstonecraft's post-French Revolution treatise, *A Vindication of the Rights of Men* (1790), and contends that it matures into an even more pointed objection to commercial bourgeois society and the impoverished state of working women in later fiction and letters.[38]

Taylor is correct to distance Wollstonecraft from conservative bourgeois feminism. Yet she overstates her case. Wollstonecraft's egalitarianism is not "uncompromising." Despite her objections to economic inequality and commercial society, Wollstonecraft accepted—and indeed integrated into the heart of her feminist vision—less visible forms of inequality on which capitalism rests. This *compromised* egalitarianism is a symptom of her comparatively restrained objection to capitalist property relations. Whereas some prominent 1790s radical democrats identified private property (and not just inequality of wealth) as an obstacle to human progress, Wollstonecraft did not. She upheld the sanctity of private property (and with that, as I explain in a moment, a class-differentiated conception of women's labour).[39]

To be clear, Taylor agrees Wollstonecraft supported private property. Wollstonecraft's "economic viewpoint," she writes, was of an "older spirit of artisanal 'independency'" that one might label "petty bourgeois."

Therefore, to call Wollstonecraft "anti-capitalist would be only partly accurate."[40] Yet it is precisely what is *inaccurate* about that statement that Taylor neglects to explore. That is, in her eagerness to distance Wollstonecraft from conservative bourgeois feminism, she doesn't attend to how Wollstonecraft's support for private property—and the inequality that implies—shapes her feminism. A close look at how women's labour figures in Wollstonecraft's feminism reveals the limits of her egalitarianism.

"Sober Pleasures" and Egalitarianism

At first glance, *Vindication* does not appear to be a treatise about work. It is, rather, an exhortation to change female *manners*. Significantly, however, it is women's proclivity to idleness and trivial preoccupations—nonwork and frivolous pleasures—that are the manners most in need of changing. "Pleasure is the business of woman's life and while it continues to be so, little can be expected from such weak beings," writes Wollstonecraft. Having forfeited reason and natural rights, women have "chosen rather to be short-lived queens than labour to obtain the sober pleasures that arise from equality."[41]

What precisely are those "sober pleasures"? What manners must women adopt if society is to be run rationally? They must learn to work. "Nature," Wollstonecraft insists, "has wisely attached affections to duties, to sweeten toil, and to give that vigour to the exertions of reason which only the heart can give."[42] The risk to women of the middle and higher ranks lies precisely in their tendency to shun hard work. Poor women (who do not have the option of shunning work), she observes, do not exhibit the same foolishness. Their ungrudging acceptance of their lot proves a model for wealthier women to emulate.

Although not ostensibly about labour, then, *Rights of Woman* nonetheless proposes a work-based prescription for women's equality. Work is, quite simply, the secret to an equal, rational civilization, one in which women qualify as citizens in their own right. For "society is not properly organized which does not compel men and women to discharge their respective duties, by making it the only way to acquire that countenance from their fellow-creatures."[43] The path to equality lies in educating women to perform their God-given duty to be sensible, *productive* people. While she expects most to undertake that duty as housewives,

Wollstonecraft sees occupations from business to midwifery as suitable pursuits for women.

This emphasis on duty and the "sober pleasures" of work prompts a reappraisal of Wollstonecraft's egalitarianism. Equality is not, in itself, a social good but a means toward a higher end: a productive, pro-work society. Or, at the very least, the two ideals—equality and duty-as-productivity—are two sides of the same coin. Wollstonecraft abjures both equal excessive wealth and equal communal wealth because they hinder industriousness. Only moderate wealth ensures people *must* work. Along with many of her contemporaries, she "lauded [the "middling life"] as the repository of all those virtues—*enterprise, independence, personal and public probity*—so conspicuously absent among both the wealthy and the impoverished."[44]

But that "middling life" and "artisanal independency," it turns out, are not self-sustaining. They require a servant class. Thus, "sober pleasures" differ for women according to their rank. This differentiation begins with their schooling. Like feminists before her, Wollstonecraft advocates equal education for the sexes but within a system already differentiated by class. After age nine, anyone "intended for domestic employments, or mechanical trades ought to be removed to other schools" that will prepare them for "plain-work, mantua-making, millinery, &c." Only those "young people of superior abilities, or fortune" should be expected to study language, science, history, and politics.[45] In other words, most poor girls are not entitled to the sort of education Wollstonecraft deems essential to promoting either economic independence and moderate wealth, or rational and free relations between the sexes.

In fact, working class women and the work they do fails to register as a *feminist* concern in the *Rights of Woman*. We see this starkly in the following passage. While commentators often note the gender division of labour it describes, it is the class division of labour here that undercuts the argument that Wollstonecraft is a strict egalitarian:

> I have then viewed with pleasure a woman nursing her children, and discharging the duties of her station *with, perhaps, merely a servant maid to take off her hands the servile part of the household business*. I have seen her prepare herself and children, with only the luxury of cleanliness, to receive her husband, who returning weary home in the evening found smiling babes and a clean hearth ... I have thought that a couple of this description, equally necessary and independent of

each other, because each fulfilled the respective duties of their station, possessed all that life could give.[46]

Taylor suggests Wollstonecraft is less beholden to capitalist class relations in her later letters and fiction. True, readers find a sympathetic treatment of working women in *Maria, Or the Wrongs of Woman*. Wollstonecraft's unfinished novel is not simply concerned with the tragedy that befalls its title character, an heiress whose abusive husband confines her to a "madhouse" after she tries to leave him. It also lets Jemima, Maria's prison attendant, tell her story of growing up in an impoverished, unloving household, and moving from one low-wage, arduous job to another.

Explicitly condemning England's marriage laws for enforcing women's subjection to men across all classes, the novel also moves beyond critiquing legal restrictions on women's lives. It portrays "the absence of respectable and profitable *employment*" as "the second greatest source of suffering of her countrywomen"—an injustice that likewise crosses class divisions.[47] Wollstonecraft thus introduces economic independence as a feminist goal. If, in her thinking, working class women don't require a revolution in female manners, she suggests through the figure of Jemima that decent work opportunities are an important aspect of their quest for freedom.

Without doubt, *Maria* strikes a progressive tone missing from the pages of *Vindication*. Jemima's choices are presented as the outcome of difficult circumstances (and the good fortune to have gained some classical education). Her strength of character and sound judgement guide and support Maria through her ordeal and ultimate escape. Yet to suggest with Taylor that this anticipates the utopian socialist feminist critique obscures the two feminisms' distinct theoretical approaches.

I discuss utopian socialist feminism in the next chapter. Here I want to stress the degree to which *Maria* is continuous with the feminism of both *Vindication* and earlier *querelle* tracts. The novel affirms rather than challenges the servile and exploitative relationship of working class to middle class women, while at the same time establishing a powerful pro-work ethos. Jemima stands out from other members of her class as stoic and unflagging in the performance of her menial and servile duties. As Maria's guard, she wields limited power over her ward but, fundamentally, Jemima functions as a helpmate: "making the bed and adjusting the room" for Maria when we first meet her, delivering meals and missives, and searching for news of Maria's child.[48] In so many ways then, Maria is not Jemima's prisoner, but her (humane and rational) mistress—a stark contrast to the brutish employers and parents of Jemima's past.

Drawing attention to working class women's labour and sympathetic to their plight, *Maria* champions a sort of moral equality between the classes. But it also naturalizes their labour. The problem, according to Wollstonecraft, is not the servile relation between rich and poor women but the extraordinarily harsh conditions and poor management of women's work—conditions that misrecognize working class women's humanity. Rather than anticipate the political-economic critique of utopian socialist feminism—a critique that examines the institutions and relations that put (a certain class of) women in the conditions Wollstonecraft laments—*Maria* advances a rational-humanist critique. That is, *Maria* frames the issue of gender inequality in terms of society's failure to recognize Jemima's humanity as a rational, autonomous individual. That misrecognition explains the inequality between two classes of women. Only the (inhumane) *conditions* of Jemima's work—of women's work—are questioned. Not their capitalist form or value.

WAGED WORK AS THE PATH TO EQUALITY

This naturalization of capitalist labour also prompts Wollstonecraft to view paid work as a potential, if partial, means of gender equality. From this perspective a decent wage is, in itself, humanizing. It can end women's dependence on men regardless of class. It follows then that women should revolutionize their manners to become good (that is, rational, stoic, duty-bound) workers—to become autonomous individuals on par with men. In this calculus, the gender division of labour is a problem only insofar as it obstructs that quest for equal participation in the labour market. The fact that the labour of creating and sustaining workers—in the first instance, domestic labour—is overwhelmingly performed by women who are either not paid or who are poorly paid is a lesser, secondary, consideration.

While Wollstonecraft explores women's relationship to the labour market by relating Jemima's story, some of her contemporaries address the issue directly. For the most part, they too view work as a means of securing women's economic independence and moral rectitude. Mary Hays, for example, suggests that educating a woman for (appropriate) trades and professions allows her to "support herself, and to acquire property," and thereby avoid marrying solely for "interest" or security.

At the same time, she stresses, women stand to gain "more firmness of mind and greater vigour of body ... [such that] many of those physical evils which afflict the female frame, in an enervated and artificial state of society, would be greatly alleviated, if not wholly removed."[49] And in a rare discussion of the double burden this arrangement imposes on women, Hays adds that those who doubt that refined women can handle so much work need only observe "the number of poor hard-labouring women with large families ... in this and in almost every other country."[50] Here again, working class women epitomize the feminist pro-work ethic.

Mary Anne Radcliffe offers an historical analysis of women's labour. Appearing in 1799, *The Female Advocate* concludes that the "grand cause" of women's poverty is men's usurpation of waged work. Women, Radcliffe notes, could once content themselves with "spinning, knitting, and preparing necessaries for the use of the family, which, being common, was not looked upon as any degradation."[51] As manufacturing and commerce expanded, the labour market also grew. But it was men, not women, who gained from this expansion. Not only did they monopolize industrial jobs, men entered occupations such as hairdressing that are, in Radcliffe's view, better suited to women. Given the dearth of respectable work, women who are otherwise virtuous and industrious have no choice but "to seek bread in the paths of vice." A better solution, claims Radcliffe, is for women to gain economic independence and respectability through their paid labour. While ostensibly addressing the lot of poor women, Radcliffe is in fact concerned with the wealthy wife or daughter who—not already accustomed to being industrious—finds herself penniless on the death of a husband or father, and thus "driven to criminal and unlawful pursuits."[52]

Priscilla Wakefield is the author of a second extended feminist analysis of work. Published in 1798, *Reflections on the Present Condition of the Female Sex; with Suggestions for its Improvement* advances a Wollstonecraftian critique of women as men's equals but socially conditioned to be indolent and indulgent. Unlike her contemporaries, Wakefield makes class distinctions an organizing principle of her study, describing the types of work and education appropriate to women in different stations of life. Lucrative employment in the arts is reserved for the first and second class of women, whose occupations must be "neither laborious nor servile" but nonetheless "productive."[53] Women in the third class are best suited for, among other things, work in retail, on farms, or in light industry (as lathe turners and toymakers, for example).

While clearly in favour of a class-based division of labour, Wakefield nonetheless extends and sharpens the feminist focus on women's paid labour. Women are excluded not just from certain occupations, she notes, but from "the most advantageous employments." And when working in similar jobs, they are paid less:

A footman ... whose most laborious task is to wait at table, gains, including clothes, vails, and other perquisites, at least £50 per annum, whilst a cook-maid, who is mistress of her profession, does not obtain £20, though her office is laborious, unwholesome, and requires a much greater degree of skill than that of a valet.[54]

Wakefield thus draws attention to women's devalued paid labour, and the inequalities *within* the labour market. Her analysis raises new questions about how the labour market is organized along gender lines, inviting a more complex feminist theory of labour—one that attends to the economic value of women's waged work (without questioning class distinctions among women).

CONCLUSION

By the 1790s feminists were grappling with the realities of women's work more directly and with greater analytic depth than ever before and laying the foundations of the equality feminist perspective. They were critical of certain economic institutions and practices restricting women from full and equal social participation, explaining women's inequality with men as a problem of irrational, authoritarian rule. Wrong-headed cultural and legal restrictions, they said, prevent women from realizing their full humanity as autonomous and *productive* beings. Despite their egalitarianism which tied women's freedom to a broader social equality, Wollstonecraft and her radical democratic feminist contemporaries based their analyses of women's work on the same rational-humanist principles that animated the *querelle des femmes*.

Without questioning the division between paid and unpaid work, or the division between women who must work to survive and those who would employ such women as servants, these feminists nonetheless point to a relationship between private and public lives of women. Barred from higher education and certain occupations, and subject to patriarchal laws and conventions, women are forced to choose between dependency on a man or poverty. A society based upon the rule of reason, they insist, would open schools and jobs to women, thereby granting women their rightful independence from men, and hence from tyranny. It would also validate women's work of childrearing and household management within the private household.

The critique of gendered expectations in education and the paid workforce, the promotion of women's financial independence, and the validation of women's labour within the household are themes tracking through the equality feminism tradition in the centuries to follow. But so too do the exclusions and contradictions of this emergent tradition—those embodied in Wollstonecraft's invocation of a maidservant to relieve the "housewife" of domestic toil, and in Hays' championing of the double burden working class women endure. Later equality feminists (as we'll see in the next chapter) address the problem of women's domestic work in alternately conventional and creative ways. But, in making equal paid labour central to their emancipatory vision, they cannot but overlook or exclude some—poor and marginalized—women. That's because the contradictions producing the double burden ultimately stem from the capitalist organization of productive relations. However important it is to morally validate women's work in the home, its distinct economic form and value in capitalist society cannot be educated or legislated away. Yearsley and Collier gesture toward an analysis of those distinct forms. But it is the utopian socialist feminists writing some thirty years after Wollstonecraft's *Vindication* who begin to forge a truly new, political economic, perspective on women's work.

3
Socialist Feminism: Two Approaches to Understanding Women's Work

In many cases the family is not wholly dissolved by the employment of the wife, but turned upside down. The wife supports the family, the husband sits at home, tends the children, sweeps the room and cooks … this condition which unsexes the man and takes from the woman all womanliness … is the result of our much praised civilization.

—Friedrich Engels, 1845

To emancipate women and make her the equal of the man is and remains an impossibility so long as the woman is shut out from socially productive labour and restricted to private domestic labour.

—Friedrich Engels, 1884

These two passages—the first appearing in Engels' *The Condition of the Working Class in England*, the second published thirty-nine years later in *The Origin of the Family, Private Property and the State*—represent an intriguing development in the famous socialist's thinking.[1] They also represent a conundrum facing nineteenth-century feminists: Is women's future to be imagined in the home or in the factory?

While the majority came down decisively on the side of opening the labour market up to women, many utopian socialists in the early decades of the century challenged the either/or premise of such a question by proposing that all women's labour, like labour in general, be radically reorganized. They argued that domestic tasks constitute *work* (as opposed to women's *duty*), laborious tasks for which women are granted little recognition and no recompense. Collective living and working arrangements would release women from these burdens, equalizing relations with men.

Many utopian socialists saw this as reason enough to extend the principles of Cooperation to women's work. However, Anna Wheeler and William Thompson arrived at the same conclusion through a different

reasoning. They applied the new "science of society" utopian socialists used to analyze production to the realm of reproduction. Women's
domestic work must be collectivized, they claimed, *because such
work contributes to the overall wealth of society.* That is, Wheeler and
Thompson departed from the rational-humanist critique that conceives
of women's responsibility for housework and childcare in terms of the
unequal burden it places on them and instead sketched the premises of a
political-economic critique of women's domestic labour. In the process,
they revealed the contradictory relation of such labour to capitalistically
"productive" labour, laying the conceptual foundation of *social reproduction feminism.*[2]

The relevance of the distinction between a moral (rational-humanist)
and scientific (political-economic) approach to the question of women's
work cannot be overstated. More than theoretical hairsplitting, it ultimately explains how and why divergent political priorities emerge within
the socialist feminist tradition. The first approach sees women's unpaid
domestic work as essential but irrelevant to the workings of capital;
patriarchal power relations exist outside capitalism, which means that
the struggle against them can only be *in addition to* the struggle against
capitalism. Feminism is thus a "special struggle" (to use Communist
Party language of a later era) that can be either carried out contempo-
raneously with or subsumed to the erstwhile "class" struggle. Wheeler's
and Thompson's political-economic approach, on the other hand, introduces the possibility that "special struggles" are at one and the same
time anti-capitalist struggles. The struggle against women's oppression
is neither optional nor contingent. It must not be sidelined if capitalism
itself is to be transformed.

This chapter begins with a discussion of Wheeler's and Thompson's
ideas, positioning their theoretical innovation within the tradition of
social reproduction feminism. Few at the time, however, truly reckoned
with the full implications of this new perspective. I consider, by way of
example, Robert Owen, the Welsh founder of the cooperative community
of New Lanark. While Owen adopts certain insights from Wheeler's and
Thompson's analysis and endorses the cooperative reorganization of
domestic labour, he fails to incorporate their specifically *feminist* critique.
I then turn to a more fulsome exploration of another early, French,
socialist feminist Flora Tristan.[3] By interweaving a political-economic
critique of *productive* labour with a rational-humanist critique of

women's inequality, Tristan inaugurates an alternative socialist feminist perspective: *critical equality feminism.*

By century's end, most liberal *and* socialist feminists embraced some version of equality feminism: the future for women, they concluded, lay in equalizing women's participation in the paid workforce, at least in the first instance. Yet neither socialist feminist perspective forged in this era shares the intense *productivist* (or "pro-work") ethos that typifies eighteenth-century equality feminism precisely because their commitment to cooperative production introduces new standards and values that determine productive activity.

THE SCIENTIFIC INSIGHT OF UTOPIAN SOCIALIST FEMINISM

With capital's nineteenth-century expansion swelling the ranks of the British middle class, the genteel women Wollstonecraft and Radcliffe addressed were no longer feminism's main audience. A managerial-professional bourgeoisie, able and anxious to define itself against the working class, formed the new economic and cultural elite. Among other things, this involved establishing at least the appearance of secure, fulfilling lives in clean, comfortable homes. For middle class women, and for mothers especially, domestic work intensified at the very time it was losing its social visibility.[4]

To be sure, middle class women didn't choose this station freely. Guided and trapped by sexist laws and prejudices, they paid for their class position in their dependence upon and submission to a patriarchal order. Yet, to forego it was to enter a world of scarcity and toil, a dependence and submission that exacted a still higher toll on women's bodies, souls, and minds. Such was the fate of most women who remained fixtures of factories, fields, mines, piecework shops, and servant quarters throughout the nineteenth century, even as the mid-century passage of protective legislation limited their hours and access to certain jobs.

In France, women mainly worked in agriculture or did piecework at home for local capitalists. Still, they comprised 40 percent of the industrial workforce, mostly in textiles, food processing and packaging, and chemicals.[5] A similar occupational breakdown is found in Britain, where in the early part of the century, most married working class women were "employed on as high or on an even higher level than working-class men," albeit for much less pay.[6] Women were also members of (male-dominated) worker organizations in such industries as glove-making, button-making, and handloom weaving, and participated in industrial struggles on both sides of the channel.[7]

Utopian socialists led much of that resistance early in the century. Blending utilitarian principles with the insistence that workers have a right to the fruits of their labour, their new "science of society" directly challenged the premises of capitalist production. Many argued that a more just and rational productive system would be based upon worker cooperation and communal ownership of property.[8] The Cooperative movement that aimed to put these principles into practice attracted thousands of women workers. Its leaders valued their participation both for the expansion of productive labour they represented and because women were seen to reinforce and foster values of love, harmony, and care upon which communalism was based.

While utopian socialism stands out within the early industrial radical tradition for its promise to emancipate men *and* women, its most influential theorists were divided as to the precise meanings and methods of women's emancipation. Charles Fourier advocated libertarian sexual relations and women's workforce participation.[9] St. Simonian leader Barthélemy Prosper Enfantin prophesied a female messiah whose powers of peace and love would lay the foundation for communal living and sexual freedom. The working class *Saint-Simoniennes* responsible for secularizing those ideas—Suzanne Voilquin, Clair Démar, Reine Guindorf to name a few—however, backed away from radical sexual libertarianism. They focused instead on reforming marriage laws and promoting economic independence while calling for women-only organizations.[10]

Robert Owen, for his part, highlighted the connection between lifelong monogamy and capitalist inequalities. Church-sanctioned marriage, he reasoned, reinforces the family form, breeding a competitive, individualist ethos, and strengthening ties to private property through inheritance. In a cooperative society, relations between the sexes could be based on love, and unions could dissolve without repercussion. Though sympathetic to women's condition, however, "Owen was not much of a feminist."[11] He saw working men and women as equally oppressed by an unjust and irrational social order organized around religion, private property, and the family.

Yet in denaturalizing social sites of women's oppression and in highlighting the ways in which economic and cultural institutions mutually reinforce social inequality and injustice, utopian socialists placed the "woman question," as it comes to be known in socialist circles, in a new light. Wheeler and Thompson considerably sharpened that thinking in *The Appeal of One Half the Human Race, Women, Against the Pretensions of the Other Half, Men, to Retain Them in Political, and thence in Civil and Domestic Slavery.* They did so by approaching women's work in the home through the same lens contemporary political economists were applying to capitalistically "productive" work. While Taylor attributes the feminism to emerge within these circles to the movement's *utopianism*—by which she means its romantic, millenarian notions of full-scale social change—Wheeler's and Thompson's central innovation to feminist theory is anything but otherworldly and idealistic.[12] It emerges, rather, from a political-economic—that is, *scientific*—approach to thinking about women's work.

The Appeal was published in 1825. Thompson's name appears on its cover, but he disavows single authorship in the introduction, insisting he is the "interpreter and the scribe of [Wheeler's] sentiments."[13] Having escaped a disastrous marriage to an Irish aristocrat, Wheeler circulated among British and French socialists, writing articles, delivering public lectures, and translating Fourier's work into English. Contemporaries described her variously as "the Goddess of Reason" and "awfully revolutionary."[14] Thompson, on the other hand, was widely considered an eccentric, a teetotalling, vegetarian, bachelor landowner in County Cork. He also authored the most extensive and influential political-economic text penned by a socialist prior to Marx, *An Inquiry into the Principles of the Distribution of Wealth Most Conducive to Human Happiness; Applied to the Newly Proposed System of Voluntary Equality of Wealth*, published in 1824.

The significance and originality of the *Appeal* is difficult to overstate. Less known today than Wollstonecraft's *Vindication* or John Stuart Mill's 1869 *Subjection of Women*, it is the most coherent and sustained feminist analysis to emerge from nineteenth-century utopian socialism, prefiguring and possibly directly shaping Mill's *Subjection*.[15] The authors take on, point by point, philosopher James Mill's contention that women have no need of political rights because their interests are subsumed in men's. The first nine chapters develop familiar arguments promoting rationalism in the face of arbitrary power, equal education and employment opportunities for men and women. They also make a forceful argument for equal political representation. Only in their "Concluding Address to Women" do they switch tracks, announcing a surprising caveat to all they have just presented: *even if* a rational system of governance replaces arbitrary rule, "still evils encompass you, inherent in the very system of labor by individual competition."[16]

Women, Wheeler and Thompson observe, contend with two physiological disadvantages making perfect equality impossible: they are weaker than men, and they bear and suckle children. Their physical frailty is of lesser consequence: as technology advances, differences in strength matter less.[17] In an age when the Pill and baby formula are as fantastical as travel to the moon, however, the authors see no way around the second disadvantage. Women's physiological capacity for childbearing and nursing encompasses "enormous physical inconveniences and pain from which men are exempt."[18]

Yet, according to the authors, the problem of inequality does not lie with these facts of biology. It lies with the competitive system that organizes the production and distribution of wealth—capitalism. That's because capitalism has no internal mechanism for accommodating those unable to work for a wage. As a result, women are forced to rely on men for their well-being. This, in turn, renders them vulnerable to man's strength and influence at home where, "Superiority in the production or accumulation of individual wealth will ever be whispering in to man's ear preposterous notions of his relative importance over woman." Meanwhile, "women's peculiar efforts and powers for the common benefit of the race are looked upon as an additional badge of inferiority and disgrace."[19] Stronger and able to be gainfully employed without interruption, men have a competitive advantage. Or, as Dolores Dooley summarizes their point:

In a capitalist society where wealth is understood in market terms, a woman's [reproductive role] was not designated a contribution to wealth. Man's superiority of earning in the market place of labour gives him a public value which is not matched by a valuing of the private sphere of reproduction and nurturing.[20]

Thus, Wheeler and Thompson conclude, a communal, cooperative system of wealth creation undercuts the tendency to gender inequality inherent in capitalism. It releases women from the individual responsibility for meeting people's subsistence needs and raising the next generation from the isolated individual household, making it instead a concern of the community as a whole.[21]

While other utopian socialists also advocated collectivization, they did not necessarily appreciate the full scope of Wheeler's and Thompson's analysis. They tended, in particular, to neglect the significance of women's reproductive activities in the overall production of social wealth. But it is precisely in highlighting *the relation of women's reproductive activities to the productive sphere* that Wheeler and Thompson theoretically clarify and deepen a general utopian socialist commitment to communal living and working. Housewives deserve to "be equally appreciated and rewarded" not just because they are doing the difficult and isolating reproductive work. They deserve as much because, like all workers, they contribute their "useful talents and efforts for the common good."[22]

Moreover, unlike many of their contemporaries, Wheeler and Thompson separate immediately biological (and therefore necessarily female) reproductive activities from those that can be performed by either sex. They calculate that women would be occupied with domestic affairs for one year (the average period for which women breastfeed their babies). After that, either men or women—"as may be most convenient"—could care for and educate children. Children, they stress, "are independent of the exertions or the bounty of any individual parent," to be maintained out of the "common stock of wealth and talents."[23]

To denaturalize women's traditional responsibilities to this degree was remarkable. Taylor tells us that "[p]rior to the Owenites, only the Pantisocratic poets had questioned women's primary responsibility for household labour and child-rearing."[24] Just as remarkable is Wheeler's and Thompson's analytical alignment of women's household tasks with paid ("productive") work. While other nineteenth-century feminists saw domestic work as women's natural or God-given duty, Wheeler and Thompson treat child-raising, cooking, laundry, and cleaning as acts of *production*—as activities involving "personal exertion of mind, skill, or muscle" which contribute to the overall wealth of society.[25] In this respect, the reproduction of people is comparable to the production of things.[26] And because, like all work, domestic work is socially organized (in private households in capitalist society), it can be socially *reorganized* (as collective labour in cooperative society).

Communal organization of reproductive work, contend Wheeler and Thompson, promotes the principles of utility, the greatest good for the greatest number: it reduces work and hardship while allowing people to perform tasks they enjoy and are good at. Not only are women spared the isolating and degrading effects of domestic chores, they are freed to contribute in other ways, according to their abilities and talents.[27] And the time devoted to domestic work also diminishes since there is less duplication of tasks. Thompson calculates this more efficient organization of labour in the *Inquiry*. He proposes that privatized housework and childcare need only consume three hours of a woman's day. But were there "a common fund for preparing their food and educating their children," one person could do the work of fifty women.[28]

Just as his contemporary nonfeminist political economists calculated the value of waged labour using a utilitarian standard, Thompson analyzes the value of domestic tasks. In the process, he glimpses a deeper insight into the value-producing mechanisms of capitalism, suggesting that the competitive system is indifferent to workers' own reproduction:

> To the capitalist, *as such*, neither the useful employment or even the existence, to say nothing of the health, moral, and happiness, of his fellow-creatures, are objects of more regard than the employment of inferior animals or machines. Besides supporting them and making themselves happy by their labor, will they yield him an average profit? If so, let them be employed. Will they not yield him an average profit? Then let them live or die as they may: with their well-being he has nothing to do.[29]

A cooperative system, on the other hand, recognizes childrearing as "an occupation more useful, not to say more necessary to human existence and happiness, than any other whatever."[30] That which the competitive capitalist system treats as private, natural, and inconsequential women's duty is in fact crucial to overall social production—morally *and* economically indispensable.

Conceiving women's domestic work as socially productive but *systemically* degraded and devalued under capitalism—and attributing women's oppression then to the *relational dynamic* between reproductive and productive work—marks a turning point in the history of feminist theories of labour. But it can be seen as such only in retrospect. At the time, this innovation failed to register beyond Wheeler's and Thompson's immediate circles. Robert Owen drew upon it fifteen years after the publication of the *Appeal* in his lectures on marriage, but in a way that dilutes its specifically feminist impulse.

Individual, private households, laments Owen, are inefficient modes of child-raising in which "one, two, three, or a-half-a-dozen children will require more care and attention to bring them up, and train them to become ignorant and vicious members of society, than would be necessary to well train and educate one hundred children." He adds:

> When [the child's] natural capacities shall be known and wisely appreciated, it will be discovered that society may train it to become, at maturity, a being of incalculable worth, capable of returning to society many hundred-fold the capital expended, and labour bestowed, in nursing and rearing it to the attainment of its full powers; that it might be made to acquire a very superior character, capable of giving and receiving the highest degree of pleasure and enjoyment, and of adding to the general stock of the wealth and general possessions of the world.[31]

In this passage child-raising is an activity that, like all productive activities, can be consciously and collectively planned. Its product, the child, is not just a future citizen, as Wollstonecraft might stress. She is a future *worker*, someone who contributes to overall social wealth.

Yet Owen does not pick up on Wheeler's and Thompson's specifically *feminist* premises or conclusions. He says nothing about the gender division of labour or the laboriousness and isolation of domestic work under capitalism. And, most significantly, while he understands women's household work as contributing to general social wealth, he does not identify any contradictory relationship between it and "productive" work. As a result, he fails to see the ways in which women's oppression is implicated in negotiating that contradiction. While Wheeler and Thompson begin their analysis by identifying women's reproductive work as disadvantaging them in the capitalist organization of labour, and Thompson further grasps capital's indifference to that work, Owen's argument (and the argument that eventually dominates the socialist tradition) revolves around the presumed superiority of a more efficient mode of production. In other words, Owen advocates collective living arrangements on grounds that have little to do with women's oppression. This conceptual blinder reappears in later socialist theorizing, bypassing a critical point about what constitutes capitalist wealth in the first place.

The central insight of social reproduction feminism, along with the *Appeal*, fades from view in the mid- to late nineteenth century. In 1840s

England, the thousands of striking women Chartists tended to frame their activism as "a militant extension of their family roles," remaining comparatively silent about the private and devalued nature of those roles.[32] Meanwhile, the movement's male leadership argued for women's withdrawal from the workforce, demanding instead a breadwinner's wage and male suffrage.[33]

Such demands reflected and fueled a cultural shift in attitudes about "appropriate" women's work, symbolized as well by Westminster passing its first piece of gender-based protective legislation in 1842.[34] The discourse of "respectability" penetrated working class culture, suggests Dorothy Thompson, with "activities as smoking and drinking … bec[oming] increasingly frowned on as relaxations for women."[35] While paid domestic work expanded throughout the nineteenth century, women lost ground to men as a proportion of full-time employment in other trades.[36]

In France too, the political influence of utopian socialism waned. Following Louis Bonaparte's 1851 coup, its feminist leaders were jailed or deported, while leadership of the working class movement devolved to an anti-feminist anarchist-socialist. Pierre-Joseph Proudhon argued for the outright exclusion of women from political society, calling the family "one of the advancements of humanity." Women, he claimed, were unable to do productive work: "If she is always sitting the blood rises, the chest is irritated, the stomach obstructed, the head heavy. If she is kept standing for a long time … she has other blood-related accidents."[37]

Traditionalist, reactionary views gained prominence at the same time as people's faith in the Cooperative movement faltered. Socialist feminists thus turned their attention to the attack on women as workers, neglecting (more than repudiating) any discussion of women's reproductive work. In sharpening their arguments for greater access to jobs and better pay, they lost sight of Wheeler's and Thompson's observation about the systemic and contradictory relation between the two forms of labour. Socialist feminists gravitated instead to a critical equality feminist analysis and politics, an approach forged in France by Flora Tristan.

FLORA TRISTAN'S SOCIALISM AND FEMINISM

Flora Tristan came of age in post-revolutionary France, well after the new regime had stamped out the brief flourishing of women's rights that had inspired Wollstonecraft. The state outlawed women's political gatherings, obliged wives to hand their wages over to their husbands, and made it practically impossible for a wife to obtain a divorce. While apprenticeship and schooling opportunities expanded for boys, girls received little formal training, finding work instead in domestic service, farms, and factories, earning about half of what men earned. Meanwhile, married middle class women, denied the right to own property, had little choice but to attend to the responsibilities of hearth and home. As in the development of English capitalism, the private, patriarchal household supported the French economy's shift from peasant and artisanal production to industrial capitalism.[38]

Under French law, Tristan was considered an illegitimate child. The state did not recognize the religious marriage in Spain of her French mother to her Peruvian aristocratic father who died when Tristan was four. Disinherited by her father's family, abused and hounded by a husband who eventually shot her in the streets of Paris (she survived with a bullet lodged near her heart), she struggled with her status as an outcast. But she also embraced it, portraying herself as a martyr to socialist and feminist causes, even while clinging to certain bourgeois sensibilities.[39] With a documentarian eye, Tristan toured Peru, England and, in the last year of her life, France, recording her impressions in notebooks, letters, and widely read books and articles.

Her goal was nothing short of leading all humanity to freedom: "I shall cause all servitude to cease in the world; I shall free women from the bondage of men; the poor from the bondage of the rich; and human souls from the bondage of sin."[40] Grandiloquence aside, Tristan was "the first person to put forward a definite plan for an all-inclusive proletarian International."[41] Her promotion of class politics based on principles of self-emancipation, internationalism, and gender equality alternately inspired and upset her radical contemporaries. And while the extent of her influence on Marx and Engels is unclear, the authors of the *Communist Manifesto* knew of her work.[42] As did the French working class. In October 1848, four years after her death and five years after the publication of *l'Union ouvrière*, thousands marched in the procession to Bordeaux's Chartreux cemetery to erect a monument in her honour.[43]

The final line on that monument's epitaph features a single word, *solidarité*, summing up Tristan's greatest political insight and provocation. Her travels had convinced her that the rich ruled everywhere through the degradation and economic exploitation of the poor. She railed against the divisions between property owners and the propertyless. Through their labour, Tristan insisted, workers create the immense wealth of their oppressors. Division and competition among workers—between the organized and unorganized, between men and women, between domestic and foreign workers—make them weak in the face of capital. The bourgeois political order could not save them. Only by uniting as workers could they take control of the wealth they produced and regain their humanity.

In *l'Union ouvrière* (1844), Tristan calls for peaceful class struggle: "The great struggle, the one which is destined to transform the social order, is that which opposes on one side property owners and capitalists ... and on the other, the workers of city and countryside who have nothing."[44] She urges workers unite to demand the right to work, education, and representation. Their union would also fund "Workers' Union palaces" to house and care for the elderly, infirm, and the very young. Recalling Fourier's *phalanstères*, Tristan imagines thousands of people living and working cooperatively, independently of capitalists. The palaces combine residence, factory, and farm, radically reorganizing labour by putting all able-bodied children, men, and women to work in accordance with their abilities. They are equally sites of training and instruction, delivering a curriculum based on principles of universalism, Christian rationalism, and public health.

Where do women fit into this picture? The short answer is: centrally. The success of the working class movement depends upon women's inclusion. But the fuller answer is more complicated, as Tristan does not formulate a coherent theory of women's oppression so much as she develops a political program based on observation and flashes of insight. In these she moves between conventional explanations of women's inequality, commentary on women's paid labour, and a feminist critique of the workers' movement.

Tristan devotes only one chapter of her short book to a discussion entitled "Why I mention Women." Addressing working class men, she briefly dispenses with the notion that *all* women are naturally inferior beings before turning to the question of *working class* women and why men should include them in the union. Here she emphasizes women's moral role in the family. Picking up on the utopian socialist reverence for women's critical emotional and intellectual guidance of their households, she insists that woman is "everything in the life of a worker."[45]

Domestic *labour* (as differentiated from work of caring, which she doesn't see as work) only registers briefly, and in a confusing way. Tristan comments that daughters are denied education in order to "share in the housework, rock the baby, run errands, or watch the soup, etc." She then compares working class parents to wealthier employer-mistresses, benefiting at the expense of their daughters' well-being: "At the age of twelve, she is made an apprentice. There she continues to be exploited by her mistress and often continues to be as mistreated as she was at home."[46]

Tristan's harsh judgement of working class mothers—she also calls them "brutal, mean and sometimes hard"—is exemplary of a more general ambivalence toward the working class. Yet, women are educable. And the workers' union and the palaces it builds are to be the means of their education. There, women are to be schooled for improvement, developing "their potential so that they can become skilled in their trades, good mothers capable of raising and guiding their children ... [while also serving] as moralizing agents for the men whom they influence from birth to death."[47]

This feminist vision is broadly consistent with Wollstonecraft's: a rational household of which women are wise managers. It is not surprising then to find passages that echo those of the earlier feminist (whom she had read and admired):

No longer considered the husband's servant at home, but his associate, friend, and companion, she will naturally take an interest in the association and do all she can to make the little household flourish. With theoretical and practical knowledge, she will employ all her intelligence to keep her house neat, economical, and pleasant ... she will put all her ambition into raising her children well. She will lovingly teach them herself, watch over their schoolwork, and place them in good apprenticeships ... Then what a contented heart, peace of mind, and happy soul the man, the husband, the worker will have who possesses such a woman![48]

For Tristan, as for Wollstonecraft, women's household "work" (though that's not the term either uses for it) is of high social value—measured on a moral, not economic, scale. Where Tristan departs from the ideals of her predecessor is in its class character. There are no servants in her scenario.[49] Also, unlike Wollstonecraft, Tristan recognizes that most women work for a wage and that their subordination to capital is especially oppressive. Although she devotes comparatively little attention to women's waged work (usually referring to "workers" as men, with wives and children), she paints a more expansive and class-conscious picture than can be found in Wollstonecraft's *Vindication* or *Maria*—one in which the source of oppression is the demeaning and brutal nature of the work, not the tyrannical boss.

Her most extensive documentation of working class life, *Promenades dans Londres*, includes a chapter on prostitution, a sympathetic treatment that suggests poverty, not morality, is the reason women take up the profession. The other notable discussion of working class women is found in *La tour de France*, Tristan's posthumously published notes. She writes here of a visit to Nîmes where she observes a public laundry, "a hole 100 feet long and forty feet deep." Tristan watches in horror as a few hundred washerwomen stand waist-deep in water polluted with soap, potash, soda, bleaching liquid, grease, and dyes to scrub and dye linens. She decries the health risks from "uterus disorders, to acute rheumatism, to painful pregnancies, to miscarriages":

> Those miserable washerwomen ... who work day and night—they who courageously sacrifice their health and their lives in the service of humanity—they who are women, who are mothers—they who have so much right to the concern of generous hearts—well, they find no philanthropists, no journalist to protest on their behalf![50]

The issue in Tristan's eyes is that women are restricted to difficult, menial labour, which they undertake for less pay than men. In a footnote to her chapter on women's rights in *l'Union ouvrière* she lays responsibility for the wage discrepancy at the feet of the capitalists:

> Workers, you have not seen the disastrous consequences that would result for you from such an injustice done to the detriment of your mothers, sisters, wives, and daughters. What has happened? The factory heads, seeing women working faster and for half pay, dismiss male workers every day from their workshops and replace them with women ... Once on this path, women are let go to be replaced by twelve-year-old children. Half-pay economy![51]

That is, according to Tristan, capitalist production thrives on pitting workers against one another, and women are valuable pawns in a game that all workers lose. This analysis identifies women's inequality as an economic experience and captures something important about the ways in which capital reinforces and sustains it. But it doesn't *theorize*, or explain, women's oppression in terms of capitalist relations. It only shows how it is that capital will use it to its advantage. The dynamic of women's oppression lies elsewhere, in cultural biases, legal discrimination or patriarchal relations at home perhaps.

Notwithstanding its class consciousness about women's waged labour, Tristan's feminism significantly overlaps with the equality feminism approach discussed in the last chapter. Both approaches ground their critique in moral reasoning: women and men partake of a shared humanity and are equally competent. As a result, they *deserve* equal consideration and treatment with men. Domestic labour may be a burden, but its relation to capitalist waged labour is not investigated. Where the two analyses diverge is in Tristan's efforts to combine this analysis with a critique of the unequal and exploitative system of capitalist economic value creation. Because capitalists use women's inequality to further exploit all workers, Tristan challenges the male-dominated workers' movement to treat women as equals. For only undivided can workers exercise sufficient political power to establish a society of plenty in which "the rich and the poor alike will work."[52] Equality between the sexes thus becomes an essential stepping-stone on the path to a society based on cooperative production.

That Tristan advances an equality feminist position alongside (and as a means of) building the political unity needed to undermine capitalism inflects her analysis with a critical edge lacking in eighteenth-century feminism—which is why I refer to this socialist feminist analysis of labour as *critical* equality feminism. At the same time, the combination of (moral) feminist and (economic) capitalist critiques suggests that two sets of power relations are in play. The tension this produces when it comes to the question of struggle is resolved in one of two related but equally unsatisfactory ways. On the one hand, Tristan appeals for class unity. This appeal has little to do with advancing feminist goals: men should accept women's equality because it strengthens the forces combating capital. The risk here is that any substantive discussion about, or action to redress, the gender inequality that fractures working class life gets sidelined. On the other hand, despite calling for unity, Tristan identifies two distinct forms of struggle, with distinct goals. Workers confront capital in the realm of production. Ending the oppression of women, however, is a task of education. These two struggles can be—*but do not need to be*—jointly undertaken.

Thus, the combination of a political-economic critique of paid labour and a rational-humanist analysis of women's unpaid work involves Tristan—as it does many socialist feminists to come—in a contradictory tangle of ideas and political commitments. So long as the socialist feminist approach to women's work is embedded in rational-humanist ideals of equality, its feminist goals are likely to either dissolve into the priorities of a narrowly defined class struggle or be treated as distinct from and additional to (but not necessarily *part of*) the confrontation with capital.

PRODUCTIVISM IN EARLY SOCIALIST FEMINISM

Given their debt to equality feminism, early socialist feminism might be expected to embrace the pro-work ethos that inflects late eighteenth-century feminism. According to Kathi Weeks, that ethos considers work "the primary means by which individuals are integrated not only into the economic system, but also into social, political, and familial modes of cooperation."[53] As discussed in Chapter 2, both Wollstonecraft and Radcliffe embrace such an ethic: while they condemn harsh conditions of paid labour, they nonetheless position work itself as a moral and economic salve for the individual, a means of personal uplift and independence. The stoic, working class woman who performs her duties without complaint (even when conditions are harsh) is a feminist heroine, an example to her indulgent, indigent, wealthier sister, precisely because she accepts her lot as worker.

Weeks notes that such liberal "mystification and moralization of work" is typical of many socialist feminists as well.[54] To what extent does it pervade the analyses of those we've just considered? Tristan, Wheeler, and Thompson are certainly "productivists" insofar as they are attuned not just to work's economic value, but its moral value too. They emphasize the intrinsic dignity of manual labour and scorn indigence and frivolity. Their model member of a cooperative society is one who, by her industriousness, contributes to the general wealth of society.

Yet, because they embed their ideas about work in a critique of capitalism, their promotion of industriousness cuts against the mystification and moralism—and individualism—inflecting eighteenth-century feminism.[55] Tristan, for example, does not call attention to the

Nîmes washerwomen in order to teach women how to bear their burdens gladly. Nor does she counsel that economic independence results from imitating their work ethic. Rather, independence for (all) women results, in her analysis, from a collective effort to reorganize the way work is performed, and how wealth is distributed. True, her Workers' Palaces are beehives of activity. But they exist to provide for the community, most especially for those *unable* to work.

Similarly, Wheeler and Thompson value work as a means of provisioning and security for all. A productive society organized on communal principles ensures everyone (and notably pregnant and lactating women) is well provided for. Guided by their utilitarian principles, they emphasize the two-sidedness of work: it is a means of pleasure and enjoyment, on the one hand, and of suffering, on the other. Indeed, they condemn women's reproductive work under capitalism precisely because they see it as unnecessarily and exorbitantly isolating and difficult. As a result, Wheeler and Thompson reserve their strongest condemnations for wasteful labour, not indigence.

These early socialist feminists do not value industriousness as a good in itself, as fortifying a person's moral fiber. Nor do they see waged work as a sufficient means of emancipating women (even if it is part of the process). What matters is organizing production and distribution such that the human needs that capitalism systemically denies can be met.

Utopian socialist feminists also laud cooperative communities for creating more, not less, leisure. Both lamenting and marveling at the technology she witnesses in England's factories, Tristan imagines the potential for machines to liberate people from manual labour:

If at first I was humiliated to see man destroyed, no longer functioning as other than a machine, I soon appreciated the immense improvement that would one day come from these scientific discoveries: brute force eliminated, manufacturing [*le travail matériel*] finished in less time, and more leisure for man to cultivate his mind.[56]

Along with limiting the amount of overall work, cooperation has the potential to make work enjoyable, aligning production with values of sociality, efficiency, security, and pleasure. Such a view emerges from the same expansive conception of labour Marx proposes—one in which work is an immanent expression of human creativity. And it speaks to the historicity of work or labour: work is neither intrinsically good nor bad; what determines work's nature are the social relations governing it.

Thus, although they embrace a pro-work ethos, Wheeler, Thompson, and Tristan do not share the same intensely moral attitude of equality feminists. Work, in their eyes, does not represent women's salvation. The problem of work is not an individual problem. It is a structural problem that must be solved collectively. And in the process of solving it, the meaning of work shifts – from a lever of oppression to an expression of freedom.

CONCLUSION

Making sense of what work means for women's freedom and oppression is the task of socialist feminism. The two perspectives to emerge in the nineteenth century—social reproduction and critical equality feminisms—both draw on the critique of political economy. But only the former extends this "scientific" analysis to the unpaid work that women do in the home.

Wheeler's and Thompson's innovation is twofold. First, they move from focusing solely on the oppressiveness of the gender division of labour to treating unpaid domestic work as integral to the system of socially productive labour. Building roads, harvesting crops, mining for coal, washing clothes, preparing meals, teaching a child to read all contribute to the wealth-creating process of society. But the capitalist system that organizes wealth creation does not accommodate women's reproductive work. Thus, in capitalist societies, the organization of such work in private, individualized households, where it is performed by women for no recompense, is fundamental to the creation of social wealth *and* an insurmountable obstacle to the realization of women's freedom.

Like Wheeler and Thompson, Tristan also insists women's freedom entails collectivizing, in Workers' Palaces, childrearing, and other household tasks. But, like Owen, she does not arrive at this position through a political-economic analysis of women's unpaid labour. Instead of attributing women's oppression to the *relation* of reproductive to capitalistically "productive" labour, she combines a political-economic critique of the latter with a rational-humanist critique of women's inequality. In embracing and developing the hybrid approach of critical equality feminism, later socialist feminists also open the door to class reductionist and/or additive political perspectives.

4
Equal Work For and Against Capital

Chapters 2 and 3 tease apart subtle but important distinctions charac-
terizing equality, critical equality, and social reproduction feminisms.
These three trajectories of feminist thought should not be viewed as
marking hard and fast divisions. As we've seen, Wollstonecraft, Tristan,
Thompson, and Wheeler share many concerns and draw, to differing
degrees, on the rational-humanist tradition which revolves around a
moral critique of women's inequality with and dependence upon men.
Nonetheless, the ways in which their analyses diverge—especially when
it comes to conceptualizing *forms* of work, and of women's work specifically—are significant. Grasping these distinctions can help reveal the
logic behind the different feminist political orientations taking shape in
the early years of industrial capitalism.

While critics tend to differentiate socialist and liberal feminisms by
their respective commitments to revolutionary and reformist politics,
the picture drawn here suggests that this is too blunt a measure. It fails
to capture the assumptions shared by both traditions and the theoretical ambiguities abiding *within* the socialist feminist tradition. On the
first point, (liberal) equality feminism and (socialist) critical equality
feminism share a commitment to the liberating possibilities of women's
waged work, even if they do so with radically different ends in mind.
They also share an essentially moral critique of household labour, identifying its arduous, isolating, and unrecompensed nature as the foundation
of women's oppression. Their political responses emphasize the need for
women to escape unpaid housework's drudgery and gain economic independence through waged work.

These similarities speak to a deeper analytic affinity: both equality
and critical equality feminisms position the relation of unpaid domestic
work to paid work as a one-way (negative) *externalized* relation. That is,
unpaid domestic work is understood as a necessary but separate form
of work, outside the processes and goals of the realm of waged labour
and capital. The central feminist problem, therefore, is that it is *gendered*
work—work for which women take near exclusive responsibility, and

which prevents them from partaking in waged work on equal terms with men.

Social reproduction feminism, on the other hand, proposes that the central feminist problem lies in the *division between two forms of work within* the capitalist system—the privatization of what is part and parcel of the overall social process of wealth creation. This perspective stresses not just the capitalist organization of unpaid domestic work, but also its *internal* and *interactive* relation to the realm of waged labour. While the fullest dimensions of that relation have only been fleshed out in the last fifty years, nineteenth-century utopian socialist feminists outlined the broad perspective, laying the essential conceptual groundwork for examining it through the lens of political economy. They applied a social scientific approach to a question that had, theretofore, been discussed in fundamentally moral terms, subjected only to a rational-humanist critique.

True, Thompson and Wheeler also mounted a moral critique that viewed domestic work as obstructive to women's freedom. But insofar as they grasped its significance to processes of overall wealth creation, they reoriented the discussion of what women's freedom and equality might look like. Rather than promoting women's independence from and equality with men through waged labour, they identified the *reorganization of all work* (such that the very distinction between productive and unproductive forms of labour dissolves) as the lynchpin of women's emancipation. Later socialist feminists—as we see in this chapter— would promote this too. But, like Tristan and Owen, they did so without embracing or developing the feminist analytic insights Thompson and Wheeler introduced.

This crucial distinction between the two traditions of socialist feminism is rarely examined. Yet if socialist feminism is to develop a coherent, nonreductionist account of women's oppression and an inclusive feminist political perspective, that distinction must be acknowledged and explored. In this chapter, I investigate the overlapping and diverging themes as they recur and develop from the mid-nineteenth to the mid-twentieth century. In short, we see liberal equality feminists begin to identify and respond to women's "double burden" of paid and unpaid work, while remaining locked within the logic—and contradictions and limits—of capitalism. Meanwhile, socialist feminists pay greater attention to women's social reproductive work than did Tristan, but they do not *theoretically* advance the analysis begun by Wheeler and Thompson. Instead, they develop the critical equality feminist perspective, working through a nascent (though problematic) theory of class and gender solidarity. They also completely fail to think through the ways in which women's work is racialized. While I consider African American women's theorization of black women's work in the next chapter, I begin this chapter with a brief review of the growing racialization of paid domestic work in order to establish the fuller historical context in which these ideas developed (and with which the theorists discussed here failed to grapple).

DOMESTIC WORK AND THE "SERVANT PROBLEM"

By the late 1800s, the rapid expansion of mechanized production, rail-roads, and communication technologies had drawn millions into waged labour throughout Britain, Europe, parts of Asia and the Americas. Not-withstanding sexist and protectionist sentiments and practices, women worked on production lines and in the service industries.[1] At the same time, those (mostly white) households that could afford to, adopted the ideals of a genteel domesticity and cleanliness, transferring the heavier, difficult, and dirty tasks feminists identified as central to women's oppression from wives and daughters to servant women and girls.

Yet, in the cities especially, relatively few local (white, native-born) girls and women were willing to cook, clean, and mind other people's children for a wage.[2] The number of white, native-born women in service in the United States, for example, fell by 40 percent between 1900 and 1930.[3] They preferred positions as shop clerks, stenographers, nurses, phone operators, and teachers—jobs that, until recently, white men had mostly filled. Less formally educated white women, meanwhile, tended to choose factory work (which had expanded as laws banning child labour came into effect) over service. Women continued to find themselves in the crux of capitalism's inability to reconcile the reproduction of labour with its rapacious hunger for labour. But how precisely they negotiated their positions as social reproducers in a racist society largely depended on their ethnic and racial background.

The racialization of domestic service was (and still is) a global phe-nomenon, bound up with colonial-imperial expansion and patterns of international migration. In Asia, Africa, and the Americas, Indigenous men, women, and children (enslaved and "free") were put to work in colonizers' homes, transplanting their employers' ideals of domestic comfort from the metropole. Some ended up travelling to Britain, where they were, for a time, considered a "fashionable luxury" in the homes of the wealthy.[4] But by the turn of the century, migrant domestic servants from less distant regions were commonplace, with Irish servants soon coming to "be viewed as indispensable to the English economy."[5] Despite their light skin tones, such domestic workers comprised a racialized "other"—their association with dirt and hard labour forming the essential underbelly of and contrast to the comfort and cleanliness of white British middle class homes.[6]

In America, racialization of domestic service developed apace, but along a somewhat different path.[7] About half the 1890 national servant workforce (and a much higher proportion in Northern cities) were international migrants. The Irish were particularly well represented, but by the 1930s most had moved on to other jobs while French Canadians worked in Vermont households, Scandinavians in Minnesota, Germans in Nebraska, and Indians and Mexicans in Arizona. Chinese "houseboys" and cooks were common in California, as were Japanese male retainers in Hawaii.[8] The Southern states alone relied on a local workforce, but notably one in which social segregation was well cemented.

If "race and domestic service were inseparable" in the South, they quickly became entwined in the North as well.[9] Between 1900 and 1920, the proportion of nonwhite female household servants in large cities tripled. And by 1944, 60 percent of domestic servants were African Americans—a fact that may partially explain the shift from live-in to live-out "help." White, native-born women returned to service in the 1930s (displacing some black women), but they remained a minority.[10]

This account makes clear that domestic service was never just a wife's work. Nor was it always unpaid. Nineteenth- and early twentieth-century black women writers and activists, whose contributions are the subject of the next chapter, highlight both these facts. Their contemporaries in the feminist and socialist movements dominated by whites, however, paid scant attention.[11] White feminists instead responded to the experiences of white women who were seeing factory, retail, and some professional and (non-domestic) service sector jobs opening up while also negotiating cultural and social pressures to be housewives.

WAGED LABOUR AND FREEDOM: THE PROBLEM OF HOUSEWORK

Calls for political representation and equal access to jobs and pay span the decades of feminist interventions and cross political lines. These

themes recur, for instance, in Harriet Taylor Mill's "The Enfranchise-
ment of Women" (1851), American feminist Charlotte Perkins Gilman's
Women and Economics (1898), and the British Women's Social and
Political Union (1903–17).[12] For with wages comes the independence
necessary to be released from men's arbitrary rule. But if women were to
gain equality, it would take something more than changing employers'
minds. They needed relief from the isolating and difficult work of caring
for house and home. Insisting that unpaid domestic labour constituted
work—and, indeed, regularly comparing it to slavery—some feminists
turned to figuring out how to release (some) women from housework's
drudgery.

American feminist Antoinette Brown Blackwell, writing in 1873, for
example, considers women to be the "natural custodians of home" but
argues for a "general reconstruction in the division of labor" so that men
can share in "the common household burdens."[13] Her proposal is part
of a larger vision in which the workday in all industries is reduced to
between three and five hours. Fifteen years later, suffragist and socialist
feminist Frances Willard pins her hopes on economic and technological
progress: "the next generation will no doubt turn the cook-stove out of
doors, and the housekeeper, standing at the telephone, will order better
cooked meals than almost any one has nowadays, sent from scientific
caterers by pneumatic tubes, and the débris thereof returned to the
general cleaning-up establishment."[14]

Some feminists called for industrial standards and regulations to be
applied at home. In an era when people "are familiar with liquefied air
and Roentgen rays ... [and] electric transit," writes Gilman, households
remain backward and unchanging sites of women's domestic servitude—
the "lowest grade of labor remaining extant."[15] The work of "heating,
lighting, feeding, clothing and cleaning" must be organized into a "large,
well-managed business combination" that ensures "regular hours of
labor and free time of rest" as well as "liberal payment for each grade of
service." Only then can "women fulfill their duties in this line and be free
human creatures too."[16]

Although willing to disrupt the gender division of labour, many
feminists were less inclined to question class or racialized divisions of
labour. Blackwell recognized that the poor are unlikely to survive on
just a few hours a day of paid labour. Her solution? Poor women should
find another job—perhaps minding another woman's children: "No
well-to-do household, where there are children under ten years ... can

afford to let the mother toil for ten hours daily ... her nursery should secure some competent and trustworthy supervision during the hours when she needs rest and change."[17] Gilman, for her part, proposed black women be trained in domestic service (and black men as farm workers) as part of a scheme to manage "negroes below a certain grade of citizenship."[18]

Clearly, not all women are to be spared the burdens of domestic labour, paid and unpaid. The question of who will do the dishes and change the diapers if women gain their independence from men by working for a wage is a persistent and unresolvable conundrum posed by the capitalist tendency to separate production and reproduction. The racial and class biases of these accounts (and the history of white flight from domestic service recounted above) reveal the extent to which the work of reproducing people is considered degrading—and thus work to be done by people that society has degraded and devalued.

WAGED LABOUR AND FREEDOM:
AN ANTI-CAPITALIST PERSPECTIVE

Having identified domestic labour as oppressive, feminists turned their attention to women's paid labour in the formal economy. Explanations of how and why waged work leads to women's freedom varied. Many left-leaning feminists became suffragists, maintaining that political representation was an essential step in gaining access to jobs, which would in turn secure women's independence from men. Others proposed collective responses, promoting vaguely worked out ideas about sisterhood. And a small minority of communitarians *and* suffragists continued to experiment with socializing the practices and spaces of domestic work.[19] But the ideas that most strongly influenced the socialist movements of the day reprise those introduced by Flora Tristan: equal work and wages place women in a better position to bring down capitalism, which will free everyone, including women.

This perspective is confirmed, developed, and popularized by German socialist and theorist August Bebel's enormously popular *Woman and Socialism* (1879), as well as by Friedrich Engels' *The Origin of the Family, Private Property and the State* (1884).[20] Bebel and Engels both argue that relations between men and women are grounded in and respond to changes in the material organization of societies. To prove his thesis, Engels draws heavily on Lewis Henry Morgan's 1877 anthropological study, *Ancient Society*. He (and Bebel picks up this argument in later editions of his book) explains that as private property supplants communal property, egalitarian clan-based systems of production and distribution break down. A patriarchal, monogamous familial system arises in order to ensure that male property owners pass their wealth on to their own offspring. This involves the "overthrow of mother right," which represents "the *world historical defeat of the female sex*. The man took command in the home also; the woman was degraded and reduced to servitude; she became the slave of his lust and a mere instrument for the production of children."[21]

Bebel and Engels also contend that while class and private property perpetuate women's oppression, capitalism draws women into the orbit of paid labour, placing a new era of equality and freedom within reach. As workers, women are degraded equally alongside men (thereby losing their "womanliness," and "turn[ing] things topsy-turvy"). Yet, at the same time, women escape "*the narrow sphere of strictly domestic life … to [fully participate] in the public life of the people*."[22] They gain economic independence from men while also fortifying the ranks fighting capital's power at the point of production. And in toppling capitalism, women and men together destroy the material base of women's oppression, private property.[23]

These socialists thus called, like equality feminists, for women's full entry into the workforce on equal terms with men. As for unpaid domestic tasks, Bebel and Engels promote the utopian socialist feminist solution: socialize them (without, however, challenging the idea that women take responsibility for them). With collective responsibility for reproducing life, women are relieved of their dependence upon men and free to participate in the "productive" workforce. They can enter freely into marriage and motherhood, or choose not to.

Although they resolve the capitalist conundrum about women's reproductive work by endorsing its socialization, Engels and Bebel introduce other dilemmas. As critics note, their "stageist" strategy (which ties the end of women's oppression to the end of capitalism) ignores sexism *within* workplaces and working class organizations, while also deferring women's struggle for equality and respect in the here-and-now for some unknowable day in the future.[24] Moreover, like Owen and Tristan, they promote the ideal of collectivizing housework without an analysis of how women's unpaid work in the household sustains the capitalist system as a whole.

Paradoxically, their exclusive focus on the gendered nature of housework leads these and other leading socialists to relegate feminist concerns with women's oppression to the backburner—conceiving of them as issues distinct from, and ultimately subsumed to, the struggles of paid workers. Here we find the seeds of socialist feminism's purported "economic reductionism" (as it comes to be known in the 1970s): the claim that socialist feminism treats all struggles that do not immediately advance the "class" struggle against capital as distractions, dismissing them as self-defeating because true and total emancipation rests on the (waged) workers' overthrow of capitalism.

Without denying the force of that critique, it is worth stressing that which is often forgotten: for Engels, Bebel, and others, the call for women to join the revolution was accompanied by a call to relieve them of the burdens of housework and childcare. That is, women, in their estimation, stood to gain something significant and real from this strategy. They were not simply asked to sacrifice feminist interests to "class" interests. The difficulty is that they had no explanation for why the socialization of housework was bound up with overturning capitalism. As a result, support for "women's issues" is treated as distinct—and therefore sepa-rable—from the general workers' struggle. This critical equality feminist approach—taken up and reiterated by individual socialists and party cadre—was to dominate for the next 150 years. And its interpreters did indeed regularly water down its *feminist* elements to a thin soup in the name of building the "class" forces of revolution.[25]

Yet not all are guilty as charged. Two early twentieth-century socialist feminists to push against that tendency are Alexandra Kollontai and Clara Zetkin. Kollontai was a member of the Russian Bolshevik Party's Central Committee prior to the 1917 revolution and became the Commissar for Social Welfare in the new government. As founder of the Woman's Department, she supported and won woman-friendly policies around abortion, divorce, and more. Zetkin was on the left of the German Social Democratic Party (SPD) and Secretary of the International Bureau of Socialist Women. She edited the women's paper, *Equality*, and organized the first International Women's Day in 1911. In 1916 she co-founded the anti-war Spartacus League, and went on to play a leading role in the German Communist Party and Third International.

Whereas Tristan, Engels, and Bebel called for gender solidarity, Kol-lontai and Zetkin engaged in practical political debate to convince party members to support the struggle for women's equality alongside and as part of the struggle for socialism. Adopting the view that women's emancipation is contingent on capitalism's destruction, they nonetheless equally contended that women's issues needed to be specifically addressed as part of that struggle—and not put off for a later day. Their efforts—which are early (maybe *the* earliest?) attempts to think through a socialist feminist theory of class solidarity—underline the difficulties of foregrounding women's issues in a socialist movement deeply committed to masculinist and gendered traditions.[26] Yet, while party members' sexism and anti-feminism obstructed those efforts, Zetkin's and Kollontai's theoretical framework did not prove fully adequate to the task they set. Notwithstanding the advances their contributions represent, they too left open the possibility that workers' and women's struggles were ultimately distinct struggles.

Kollontai and Zetkin stress that women's experiences of oppression vary by class position and that working class women's oppression is integral to the very conditions that sustain the lives of wealthy women. Because families must fend for themselves under capitalism, *all* women are dependent upon their husbands and therefore vulnerable. They thus supported the demands of the mainstream women's movement for equal access to training and paid work. "The question of women's emancipation is the question of work," writes Zetkin. "Just as workers are subjugated by the capitalists, women are subjugated by men and they will continue to be in that position as long as they are not economically independent."[27] Kollontai is equally adamant: "only by taking this path [of paid labour] is the woman able to achieve that distant but alluring aim—her true liberation in a new world of labour … step by step she transforms herself into an independent worker, and independent personality, free in love." And free, she adds, to fight "in the ranks of the proletariat."[28]

To a point, according to Kollontai and Zetkin, the interests of working class and wealthier women converge. But only to a point: whereas middle class women can rest content with economic independence, the problems working class women face are more deeply rooted in the capitalist system. Capitalism, they observe, degrades all workers and uses women's lower wages relative to men to intensify that degradation. Moreover, those low wages make women's responsibilities at home that much harder. As Zetkin explains:

The proletarian woman has gained her economic independence, but neither as a human being nor as a woman or wife has she had the possibility to develop her individuality. For her the task as a wife and a mother there remain only the breadcrumbs which the capitalist production drops from the table.[29]

The enemy is not men, nor unfair employers even. It is capital. "Equal rights ... are, for proletarian women, only a means of advancing the struggle against the economic slavery of the working class."[30]

From those breadcrumbs working class women feed and clothe their families and raise their children. And while Kollontai and Zetkin bemoan the hardships involved in such work, neither analyzes the significance of domestic labour to wider processes of wealth production. In their eyes, women's work at home is burdensome (and must be socialized), but it has no *economically significant productive function*. Rather, as capitalism consolidates, writes Kollontai, "the marital/family union develops from a production unit into a legal arrangement concerned only with consumption."[31] Women's domestic labour is thus largely superfluous. "The machine superseded the wife. What housekeeper would now bother to make candles, spin wool or weave cloth? All these products can be bought in the shop next door."[32] Zetkin seems to agree: "Large-scale industry has rendered the production of goods within the home unnecessary and has made the domestic activity of women meaningless."[33]

But neither socialist feminist entirely dismisses the wider social value of domestic work—at least when it comes to creating a communist society. In an 1896 speech to the SPD Congress, Zetkin urges that party propaganda encourage women "to carry out these tasks [of wife and mother] better than ever in the interests of the liberation of the proletariat." The notetaker at that meeting records "Vivid agreement" from the audience when she continues, "Many a mother and many a wife who fills her husband and children with class consciousness accomplishes just as much as the female comrades that we see at our meetings."[34]

Kollontai extends that argument to the post-revolutionary, transitional, phase of Bolshevik rule. As a leading member of that state, she oversaw the establishment of creches, maternity homes, children's clubs, and communal kitchens, all intended to reduce women's responsibility for the home. But she also argued that maternity itself is a social obligation:

The social obligation of the mother is above all to give birth to a healthy baby. The labour republic must therefore provide the pregnant woman with the most favourable possible conditions; and the woman for her part must observe all the rules of hygiene during her pregnancy, remembering that in these months she no longer belongs to herself, she is serving the collective, "producing" from her own flesh and blood a new unit of labour, a new member of the labour republic. The woman's second obligation is to *breast-feed* the baby; only when she has done this does the woman have the right to say that she has fulfilled her obligations.[35]

Kollontai's clear willingness to sacrifice women's bodies to the state might seem highly naïve and possibly alarming. But it appears less so if the reader appreciates that she, first, presumes a genuinely democratic state where women have a collective and equal voice in creating maternalist policies; second, stresses that the state *educates* (rather than forces) women to comply; and third, believes maternity itself is transformed under socialism. Whereas capitalism is hostile to maternity and bad for women's and children's health, under socialism women's reproductive tasks are fully supported: "Maternity is no longer a cross. Only its joyful aspects remain; only the great happiness of being a mother, which at the moment only the [wealthy] Mashenka ladies enjoy."[36]

Regardless of how we judge this discussion, it is clear that Kollontai in particular has some notion that women's reproductive labour figures in the economic well-being of a society—at least in a communist society. That is, she picks up on the thread spun by Thompson and Wheeler that assigns an economic function to women's domestic work. But she doesn't develop this line of thought, instead resting her case for feminism on a rational-humanist critique that foregrounds the burdens of domestic labour and urges women's economic independence as a path to equality and as a necessary step on the longer path to freedom.

CONCLUSION

These founding texts of the dominant socialist feminist tradition treat women's unpaid work in the home as a key component of women's oppression. Yet this theme is common to all three feminist approaches to thinking about labour. The distinction between both versions of equality feminism, on the one hand, and social reproduction feminism, on the other, is not whether domestic labour is a site of oppression. It is how that labour is theorized in relation to capitalistically "productive" labour.

And despite some provocative statements, Engels, Bebel, Kollontai, and Zetkin fail to seriously engage with a political-economic conceptualization of unpaid domestic labour.

They do, certainly, identify the division of productive and reproductive spheres that typifies capitalist society as a structural component of capitalism—a division that ultimately devalues the work women do. But they don't investigate the peculiarly *capitalist* devaluation of domestic labour. They do not, that is, examine how the degradation of that labour and of the women who do such work features as part of the edifice that sustains private property and capitalism. Instead, they suggest that the material basis of women's oppression is the presence of private property and an uninvestigated tendency for men to pass that property on to their biological heirs; and the gender division of labour that attends the separation of productive activities from reproductive activities.[37]

Housework and childrearing in their estimations are necessary labour, but they are necessary to *life*, not to the workings of *capital*. While essential to life, unpaid domestic work figures conceptually solely as a burden, unfairly relegated to women who then lack the time and energy for paid, "productive," labour. Thus, the gender division of labour— not the relation of unwaged domestic work to waged work—is the key feminist problem, responsible for women's dependence on men. *Dependency* in this view is the essence of women's oppression, and women's equal treatment as workers is the feminist solution to that problem. Their (additional) struggle as workers is the socialist solution to a related but different, class, problem. And the socialization of housework reconciles "the woman question." It doesn't reconcile the problem of class society.

Two political conclusions follow from this analysis—neither of which are anticipated nor consciously promoted by those who established critical equality feminism as the dominant socialist feminist perspective in the nineteenth century. First, given that the two sets of power relations are fundamentally different in nature, a dualist strategy of struggle makes sense. The feminist struggle is for equality within the system; the class struggle is to overturn the system. Each enjoins distinct subjects (women *versus* workers) and pursues distinct goals (equality *versus* communism). The feminist struggle is a *prelude* to the class struggle (insofar as it is required if women are to be paid workers), but it is not necessarily *part* of it.

Second, it is unclear how exactly the socialization of domestic work figures in this analytic. It is alternately a *means* to a greater end (insofar as it facilitates women's entry into the labour market); or a logical exten-sion of socialist principles (and therefore made possible by successful class struggle.[38] One thing is for sure: it is not the goal or telos of either feminist or class struggle. As a result, it (and feminism more generally) can be—and indeed was often—considered optional to overturning capitalism. If women can enter the workforce without the full-scale socialization of housework and childrearing (as they do now, for instance) or without being fully equal to their male co-workers (as is also still the case), then the class struggle can carry on whether or not sexism is challenged. After all, the stageist, economic reductionist logic in play already suggests women could logically defer their demands. Is it too much of a stretch for them to defer the socialization of domestic labour until after the revolution as well? Such are the pitfalls of the critical equality feminist perspective.

5

Anti-Racist Feminism
and Women's Work

The traditions of feminism discussed in the last chapters searched for answers to what was increasingly being called "the woman question." But, as critics have long pointed out, the feminist "woman" was not everyone's woman. While she might be specified as working or middle class, she was invariably a white woman. Even American and British feminists involved in the abolitionist movement failed to seriously think through the link between their two causes. Neither did Engels, Bebel, Kollontai, or Zetkin connect their scathing critiques of imperialism, colonialism, and slavery to woman's oppression in capitalist societies. And yet, as the last chapter recounts, the racialization of women's work was central to their very object of critique. Not surprisingly, black feminists did take note.

This chapter looks at ideas black feminists developed over the same period as the liberal and socialist white feminisms just discussed. Activists and theorists as diverse as Sojourner Truth, Anna Julia Cooper, Sadie Alexander, and Claudia Jones all wrote and spoke about racism, women, and work, implicitly challenging the assumptions and political direction of white feminist analyses.[1] Most significantly, they refashioned the very concept of domestic labour. They did not single-mindedly associate it with motherhood and full-time unpaid housework (which few black women could genuinely choose as a singular occupation in any case). Instead, they identified domestic labour with servitude—that is, with the extension of racialized work from slavery to waged labour. As with most black women (married or not) working for a wage, black feminists had few illusions that entry into the workforce would grant them freedom and independence. It was the *terms of entry* that bothered them—the racialized, servile nature of (paid) domestic and other forms of menial labour. Women's struggle for freedom, in this perspective, is inextricably tied to the struggle against racism.

A full consideration of the theorization of black women's labour is the subject for a book in itself. In sketching its contours, this chapter aims to reveal how black feminist theories of work during this period challenge certain premises of equality, critical equality, and social reproduction feminisms while also adopting and extending these same traditions of feminist thought. Those whose ideas align with equality and critical equality feminist frameworks understood that not all waged labour is equal in a racist society, but they still saw equal education and employment as central means of reaching their feminist, anti-racist goals. Others advanced ideas that aligned more with social reproduction feminism, emphasizing the integrated nature of oppression and exploitation. These theorists deepened and complicated the conception of domestic labour at the heart of that analysis, creating a space for a theory of women's labour that moves beyond that trajectory's narrow focus on gender and class. That it takes decades for socialist feminist analysis to return to these insights is symptomatic of the racism inscribed in the most influential political and intellectual traditions of the left.

BLACK WOMEN'S WORK

In the United States, the history of slavery ensured that African American women's experiences of marriage and motherhood had little in common with the privatized, individualized domesticity taken for granted by white feminism. During slavery, gender relations in black households appear to have been comparatively egalitarian. Historians offer two main explanations for this fact. Like the feudal peasants discussed in Chapter 1, interactions between enslaved men and women were shaped in the first instance by their shared experiences of domination. The power exercised over them by the plantation owner, his family, and overseers tended to undercut black male authority over their wives and children.

Second, slavers had wrenched African Americans from Indigenous communities organized around relatively egalitarian gender relations in which women's work was socially valued. The recently enslaved thus drew on traditional mores of mutual respect and dependence, which they held in living memory, when organizing their own plantation-based communities. This egalitarianism recedes, however, after the Civil War when those communities broke up and more fully privatized households became the norm. Yet these more equitable impulses do not completely vanish, and they are further reinforced in the postbellum era by the respect and authority accruing to black women whose income from waged labour was often essential to a family's survival.[2]

Historically, African American women have also taken primary responsibility for caring for children, tending the sick, preparing meals, and washing clothes. But their experiences of this work differed in significant ways from white women's. On the one hand, most enslaved people had little time for and control over the conditions of domestic life, and they reared children with the bitter knowledge that the lives they were reproducing were not, or were unlikely to ever be, free lives. On the other hand, what time and energy they expended on such tasks was often organized collectively, among multi-generational networks of unrelated women. And, Deborah Gray White stresses, time spent sustaining themselves and their households tended to be valued as time not given to the "master"—an assertion of their humanity in the face of deeply dehumanizing forces.[3]

After emancipation, a good proportion of black women withdrew from the (formal) labour force—though the extent of this is difficult to determine.[4] It is unlikely they did so in aspiration of white middle class lifestyles as some historians have suggested. Rather, given abysmally low wages, staying home to grow food to sell or feed the family simply made good survival sense.[5] It also placed women in a better position to defend the integrity of their recently won freedom. Leslie Schwalm documents how freedwomen on South Carolina rice plantations "negotiated and reconstructed plantation and domestic labor ... defend[ing] the new autonomy of their families and household economies from exploitation by planters and unwelcome intervention by northern agents of Reconstruction."[6] That said, by the turn of the twentieth century, most black women earned a wage. A few found manufacturing jobs, and many in the South laboured in fields. But the dominant occupation, North and South, was domestic service performed for middle class, white, households.[7]

"RACE" CONSCIOUSNESS AND EQUALITY FEMINISM

It is not surprising then that feminists addressing the oppression of African American women would see work as a "core" issue.[8] As early as 1831, Maria Stewart asked: "How long shall the fair daughters of Africa be compelled to bury their minds and talents beneath a load of iron pots and kettles?"[9] No girls, she says in an historic speech the following year to an audience of black and white abolitionists, "have enriched themselves by spending their lives as house domestics, washing windows, shaking carpets, brushing boots, or tending upon gentlemen's tables."[10] In step with equality feminism, Stewart attributes the relegation of black women to such jobs to prejudice, ignorance, and dependency, all problems deepened by black people's poverty. She urges that schools be built to allow women to pursue their moral and scholarly improvement such that they can avoid the "horrors of servitude," find careers and become community leaders.[11] (Thirty-five years later, Sojourner Truth put a slightly different spin on black feminism's urgings about work. "I have done a great deal of work, as much as a man, but did not get so much pay," she proclaimed to a women's rights convention. "What we want is a little bit of money."[12])

Later black feminists continued to stress the convergence of feminist and racial causes: access to better paid, non-servile careers is touted as the path to equality and elevating the standards of black life in America.[13] Anna Julia Cooper, an enslaved domestic servant who became a civil rights activist and educator, made this very point in her 1892 book *A Voice from the South*.[14] According to Cooper, women are uniquely capable of bringing moral considerations to bear on religion, science, art, and political economy. To do so, however, requires that they enter the halls of higher education, as equals of men and whites. Meanwhile, journalist and women's rights crusader, Gertrude Mossell, devoted the first twenty pages of *The Work of the Afro-American Woman* (1894) to listing by name black women educators, lawyers, doctors, dentists, business owners, artists, and more—all with university and college degrees. This she presents as evidence against the racist depiction of black women as lazy. "The women of this race have always been industrious," insists Mossell, "however much the traducers of the race may attempt to make it appear otherwise."[15] By the century's end, many activists were taking up Stewart's call, promoting and founding training schools for industrial and domestic service jobs, as well as organizing black women workers through "wage-earner associations."[16]

This push to better integrate black women into the paid labour force did not, however, imply a wholesale acceptance of the wider economic system. Like radical democratic feminists one hundred years earlier, certain nineteenth-century black feminists challenged the principles and ethos of an economic regime based upon the accumulation of individual wealth. Cooper directly links economic excesses to the degradation of her "race":

The desire for quick returns and large profits tempts capital offtimes into unsanitary, well nigh inhuman investments,—tenement tinder boxes, stifling, stunting, sickening alleys and pestiferous slums; regular rents, no waiting, large percentages,—rich coffers coined out of the life-blood of human bodies and souls ... These are some of the legitimate products of the unmitigated tendencies of the wealth-producing period.[17]

Women, she adds, must be counted on to temper "the cold, mathematical, selfishly calculating, so-called practical and unsentimental instinct of the business man."[18]

Like some white feminists of their era and before, some nineteenth-century black feminists embraced maternalist views of womanhood—views that naturalize the gender division of labour, pointing to it as proof of women's positive moral worth and social role. Stewart, for example, sees no contradiction in promoting careers for women and urging them to "strive to excel in good housewifery, knowing that prudence and economy are the road to wealth."[19] Similarly, Cooper advocates higher education for girls not just to grant them greater self-reliance. She also thinks it will make them "better mothers and housekeepers."[20] And Fannie Barrier Williams lauds the efforts of associations that teach African American women "how to make the homes of the race the shrines of all the domestic virtues rather than a mere shelter."[21]

In many respects, then, these texts and speeches tread a familiar (if not identical) equality feminist path: promoting education and waged work as a means of improving women's position; suggesting that excessive inequality of wealth more generally has something to do with social oppression; and at times uncritically accepting the gender division of labour that grants women responsibility for domestic matters. The language of "racial uplift" partially substitutes for the white equality feminist language of independence—perhaps because black women knew too well that earning a wage was not enough in itself to improve their situation. Yet, (non-servile) waged work, and the educational opportunities required to prepare for such jobs, are nonetheless the central paths to justice for these black feminists. As such, this era's black feminism shares with equality feminism a rational-humanist framework of critique that posits an ideal of equality among autonomous individuals.

On the other hand, the specter of Stewart's fair daughters of Africa buried beneath a load of iron pots and kettles is never far from view.

In this respect, nineteenth-century black feminists forged a new path. Rather than stress the oppressiveness of unpaid reproductive labour, black feminists largely focused on the difficult conditions and the degradation black women experience in the paid labour force—particularly, in paid domestic service. For Stewart, servitude is a fate worse than death, while Williams considers menial labour to carry "the stain and meanness of slavery."[22] And Cooper condemns the invisibility of the "pinched and down-trodden colored women bending over [other, white, people's] washtubs and ironing boards—with children to feed and house rent to pay."[23]

While they too do not resolve the question of who cleans, feeds, and nurtures the family when women are in the paid workforce, their insistence that racial and gender oppression are entwined cuts against a go-to middle class white feminist resolution. That is, black feminist "race" consciousness means they are unlikely to imagine women's freedom as contingent on having "merely a servant maid to [perform] the servile part of the household business."[24]

RACIALIZING FEMINISM: RETHINKING DOMESTIC WORK

In the first decades of the twentieth century, black feminists advanced more rigorous analyses of black women's labour. Beverly Guy-Sheftall identifies Elise Johnson McDougald as the first essayist to articulate, in 1925, African American women's "double burden of racism and sexism."[25] McDougald also draws attention to some of the complexities of that burden, noting that not all African American women share in it equally. She lists, without elaborating, four categories of women workers, differentiating (i) a "group weighty in numbers struggling on in domestic service" from (ii) "a very small leisure group," (iii) women in professions and trades, and (iv) the "even less fortunate fringe of casual workers."[26]

Five years later, Sadie Alexander—the first African American woman to earn a doctorate in Economics (in 1921)—focuses on a category McDougald doesn't even consider. She celebrates the remarkable increase in the number of black women factory workers in an article for *Opportunity*, a sociology journal that helped foster the Harlem Renaissance. The 100-fold increase between 1910 and 1920 in black women's manufacturing jobs (compared to a 1 percent increase among white women), she proposes, permits "Negro women ... a greater degree of self-respect and ... opportunities for social intercourse and expression that as domestic servants were denied them." Domestic servants, she continues, are denied dignity because:

> Standards of value are money standards [in the industrial capitalist] new economic order ... Modern industrial processes, having robbed the home of every vestige of its former economic function, left in the home to be performed by the woman only those services which are as "valueless" and "priceless" as air and water but are not recognized as *valuable* in the price economy."[27]

As for factory work, Alexander observes, black women's labour is also devalued. All women are "marginal workers" earning lower wages than men, but black women make less than both men and white women performing the same jobs. This wage differential, she argues, is critical to capitalist productivity: it may not be "the efficient cause of the mass production," but "without this available labor supply, at a low price, mass production in many industries would not have been undertaken."[28] Although Alexander urges workers to overcome "racial friction," she does not attribute these low wages to racism. It is simply, she claims, "the natural process of events in history" for a "new and inexperienced nationality, sex, or race" to start at the lower rungs and pay scale, occupying those jobs "vacated by an earlier stratum of workers who have moved on to more alluring places."[29]

Despite gesturing toward a more critical perspective by thinking through the question of value in relation to domestic work, then, Alexander endorses the equality feminist path to black women's liberation: if society values productive work and not domestic work, women need to move from the home to the factory. Once in the door, they "must eventually push on to more skilled, better paying jobs."[30] She too leaves the problem of who will clean up the messes at home and feed the children unresolved (saying only that the increase in household income will offset any negative effects at home).

Alexander departs from the equality feminist perspective, however, on two counts. First, she emphasizes that the productive realm is dependent upon racialized and gendered wage discrimination, second, she conceptualizes improved conditions for women as an escape from the isolation and hardship of *paid* domestic work. In both these ways, she complicates the conception of women's work, raising a new set of questions that call for more nuanced critique. Specifically, her analysis leads one to ask why paid domestic work is undervalued and racialized, and how are those two aspects of it related.

"RACE," CLASS, AND GENDER: THEORIZING TRIPLE OPPRESSION

African American feminists in the American Communist Party (CPUSA) began to develop answers to such questions. While promoting improved conditions of women's waged work, they paid greater heed to paid and unpaid domestic labour. In so doing, Bill Mullen argues, they grasped—if not fully theorized—the integral relation of racialized social reproductive work to capitalism. Mullen identifies Louise Thompson Patterson's 1936 article for the party's women's journal as "a pioneering moment in analysis of black domestic work as a nodal point within capitalism."[31] In it, Patterson sketches a scene of Northern and Southern US black women shifting in and out of waged and unwaged work from dawn till dark. In New York, women pour off subways and arrange themselves at the "Bronx 'slave-market'" where "thrifty 'housewives'" descend to drive a hard bargain with "the most exploited section of the American working class—the Negro woman." Patterson, who was likely the first to use in print the term "triple exploitation" in relation to black women workers, goes on to applaud the broad-based, anti-racist class politics aimed at organizing domestic workers, professional women, and housewives (around rent and schooling) that she sees emerging.[32]

Claudia Jones, a Harlem activist and the only black woman to sit on the CPUSA's central committee, extends the analysis of triple exploitation.[33] In a 1949 article for the party journal, *Political Affairs*, she invokes the history of slavery to understand both past and present forms of black women's labour. Presenting an alternative interpretation to a core white feminist concept, she argues that enslaved women's responsibility for their own households was empowering: "The Negro mother was mistress in the slave cabin … her wishes in regard to mating and in family matters were paramount."[34] After the end of slavery, she notes, legal measures and the scattering of communities into independent households subjected women more directly to their husband's authority. But their wider political, social, and economic role was not fully undermined since they often became the family breadwinner and remained active within their wider communities.

Slavery's legacy also centrally shapes black women's waged work, observes Jones. Excluded "from virtually all fields of work except the most menial and underpaid, namely, domestic service," black women workers were likely to end up—just as in the days of slavery—in servitude to whites, relieving middle and upper class white women in particular of the dirtiest, most labour-intensive tasks associated with housewifery. For this reason, she contends, "the struggle for jobs for Negro women *is a prime issue.*" But not just any jobs. The struggle must be one "against the growing practice of the United States Employment Service to shunt Negro women, despite their qualifications for other jobs, only into domestic and personal service work."[35] Here, Jones sounds much like earlier black feminists advocating racial "uplift" through improved career opportunities. But her theorization of women's work, and how that work features in women's oppression and liberation, is at once more complex and wide-ranging than earlier black feminism. To begin, she picks up on the CPUSA's dominant strain of critical equality feminism, albeit with a constant eye on the racial dynamics of the labour market. At the same time, Jones' analysis lends important insight into the complex nature and scope of social reproductive labour—insights that social reproduction feminists only much later integrate into their framework in developing an analysis of capitalism as a thoroughly racialized as well as gendered production system.

To turn first to the ways in which Jones' theorization of women's work fits with and advances the critical equality feminist tradition that steered CPUSA policies on "the woman question." In a 1949 article, "We Seek Full Equality for Women," Jones repeats what had by then become a socialist truism, that women's oppression stems from their relationship to the "mode of production." Citing Engels, she writes, "the woman question [is] a special question *which derives from the economic dependence of women upon men,*" and likens this dependence to that of the proletariat (wife) on the bourgeois (husband). The goal, writes Carole Boyce Davies in an introduction to a reprint of that article, is "to free woman of household drudgery, … win[ning] equality for women in all spheres."[36] And in *Political Affairs*, Jones emphasizes that as equals in the paid workforce, black women can join the frontlines in the class struggle against capital:

> To the extent that the cause of the Negro woman worker is promoted, she will be enabled to take her rightful place in the Negro proletarian leadership of the national liberation movement and by her active participation contribute to the entire American working class whose

historic mission is the achievement of a Socialist America—the final and full guarantee of women's emancipation.[37]

Jones adopts *and* advances the critical equality feminism understanding of labour here. She adopts it insofar as she draws on the rational-humanist critique that positions domestic labour as a burden unreasonably placed on women's shoulders—a burden to be escaped through gaining equality with men in the workforce. But she advances that understanding by introducing two complications. First, "household drudgery" refers to both unpaid and paid labour. Second, Jones never loses sight of the racism that relegates black women to servile paid labour and makes their equality as workers so elusive. For these reasons, she insists that the CPUSA and feminists take up the struggle against racism—whether that struggle unfolds on the shop floor or in the community.[38]

Yet Jones' conception of domestic labour is even more complex and more central to her analysis than her views described above suggests. She notes the reliance of households on the working class wage, linking black women's low wages to the ghettoization of African American lives more generally:

> The conditions of ghetto-living—low salaries, high rents, high prices, etc.—virtually become an iron curtain hemming in the lives of Negro children and undermining their health and spirit! ... Little wonder that one out of every ten Negro children born in the United States does not grow to manhood or womanhood!"[39]

And it is the black woman who, "as mother, as Negro, and as worker fights against the wiping out of the Negro family." Along with often being the family's main breadwinner, they work collectively to respond to these degrading conditions: "2,500,000 Negro women are organized in social, political and fraternal clubs and organizations ... [which] play a many-sided role concerning themselves with the economic, social and political life of the Negro ... family." Much more than mere "charity work," they are engaged in providing education and other social services to a community devastated by the "Jim-Crow lynch system in the U.S."[40]

Jones thus identifies and celebrates a broad view of black women's social reproductive labour—one that is not restricted to the domestic sphere but is nonetheless crucial to the overall processes of life-making. And, she stresses, all this is carried out by members of a "triply-oppressed" group. The very notion of black women's triple oppression ("as mothers, as Negros and as workers") suggests capitalism's boundlessness.[41] It suggests that capitalism does not just organize our workplaces. It organizes our living conditions too. In this way, Mullen argues, Jones "centers social reproduction analysis as hermeneutic ... as an explanatory framework for diagnosing and challenging capitalism in totality."[42]

CONCLUSION

The anti-racist feminists considered in this chapter all reprise the three trajectories of feminist thinking about women's work traced in this book. They also extend those perspectives in ways that more accurately and fulsomely capture the capitalist organization and domination of productive and reproductive labour—in ways, that is, that capture its racialized, patriarchal nature. And it is Claudia Jones who most clearly and insistently articulates a political perspective that Angela Davis retrieves and, as one among others in the 1960s and 1970s, develops: that the fight against capitalism is also a fight against racism and sexism. That is, Jones and Davis do not restrict their vision of class struggle to the workplace and issues arising from waged work. Black women fighting for justice in their communities are central actors in class struggle—anti-racist feminists, whom the party, they contend, should support. Unfortunately, the party, as we see in the next chapter, did not follow this logic. Not only was it deeply committed to a watered-down version of critical equality feminism, it drove the one person who seriously engaged with a social reproduction feminist perspective—Jones' white contemporary, Mary Inman—out of its ranks.

PART II

SOCIAL REPRODUCTION FEMINISM

6

A Political Economy of "Women's Work": Producing Patriarchal Capitalism

As should be clear by now, the gender division of labour figures centrally in liberal and socialist feminist explanations of women's oppression. But it does not figure in the same way across the three trajectories I've outlined. For equality and critical equality feminisms, *gendered labour itself* is the problem to be resolved and not the system that governs it. Social reproduction feminism, on the other hand, identifies *the organization of capitalist production*—the outcome of which is gendered labour—as the key obstacle to women's freedom. This chapter addresses twentieth-century socialist feminist attempts to retrieve and develop the latter perspective primarily through the work of Mary Inman, Margaret Benston, Sheila Rowbotham, and the theorists who inspired the international Wages for Housework campaign.

Before discussing their contributions, however, summarizing the distinction between the trajectories' positioning of gendered labour may be helpful. Both equality and critical equality feminisms identify women's dependence upon men as the essence of their oppression, attributing that dependency, in turn, to the *nature of the labour women do*. In other words, women's relegation to work that is difficult, isolating, and under-valued makes them dependent upon men who are "free" to do the sort of work that commands a wage. Women's independence and eventual freedom therefore requires transcending the gender division of labour. This centrally involves reforming access to education and training, and relieving women of unpaid and undervalued work—measures aimed at promoting their entrance onto the waged labour market on equal terms with men.[1]

Critical equality feminism begins with this analysis but adds a further dimension. It stresses that women's oppression is historically entangled with the emergence of capitalism—specifically with the tendency to hive off reproductive labour from the times and spaces of capitalistically "productive" labour. The problem then is not simply gendered labour; it is *gendered labour in capitalist societies*. Along with denaturalizing relations between men and women, this historical perspective brings the issue of economic value into sharper focus, leading to an important analytic insight: women's work in the home is devalued economically because, *for the capitalist*, it holds no value: it is not "productive" labour that capital directly dominates in order to accumulate more capital. Because it is "unproductive," women's unpaid domestic work is a matter of *political* oppression, external to the functioning of the economic system.

Women's entry into waged work is thus a step on the path to equality and independence. But it is also an entry into society's processes of value creation, an opportunity for women to participate in the capitalist system. And, crucially, it is an entry into the spaces of confrontation with capital. Because the privatization of domestic work prevents women from joining the paid workforce, it must be socialized. And only when it is fully socialized under a system of communal wealth will women be fully free—free of isolated, difficult work and free to be productive members of society. While the structural relationship of unpaid to paid labour is, according to critical equality feminism, a problem, *it is not what generates or sustains women's oppression*. Rather, the focus of *feminist* critique here is the devalued nature of women's unpaid domestic work.

Social reproduction feminism distinguishes itself from both foregoing approaches in that it does not treat women's oppression as stemming from the nature of their unpaid domestic labour (however much it sees housework as a symptom of oppression). Rather, it attributes women's oppression to *the position of such work relative to paid work, and its contribution to the overall social process of wealth creation*. Granted, domestic labour is arduous and may be "unproductive" of capitalist value.[2] And, granted, women's overwhelming responsibility for housework and childcare generally makes them dependent upon men. But this is not the full story of their oppression.

The fuller explanation involves exploring how unpaid domestic labour and capitalistically "productive" labour *interact* to sustain a society dominated by capital. Women's oppression is thus a feature of the very anatomy of capitalist productive relations—specifically, of the capitalist-prescribed *reconfiguration of the relation between* paid and unpaid forms of work. Grasping the dynamics of that relation—of the ways in which both forms of work are separate but interconnected parts of a social whole—is critical to understanding, and figuring out how to end, women's oppression in capitalist societies. In pushing beyond the fact that women's unpaid work at home is typically hard, isolating, and responsible for women's dependence upon men, social reproduction feminism grapples with the *systemic* nature of women's oppression in capitalism.

Critical equality feminism also identifies a systemic link between these sets of social relations. But it asserts and describes their integration without adequately explaining the dynamics sustaining it. The insight that women's work in the home is devalued because it lacks value to the capitalist does not tell us why—or if—capital *must* devalue that work. As for how these two kinds of work interact to reproduce our society, critical equality feminists have tended to default to a functionalist logic, explaining gender relations as shaped by the demands of capital to keep wages as low as possible (by having housewives available as a reserve army of labour).

Alternately, social reproduction feminism proposes a complex, necessary, and contradictory interaction, arguing that *patriarchal relations both shape and are shaped by the economic dynamics of dispossession and accumulation.* Yet it is only in the twentieth century that social reproduction feminism emerges as a coherent trajectory of feminist thought. Anna Wheeler and William Thompson lit the spark by conceptualizing unpaid domestic work as part of the general creation of wealth and including it within a political-economic critique of capitalism. While many later socialist feminists identified women's social reproductive labour as oppressive, only a few extended this radical insight into their analyses. Alexandra Kollontai did when she discussed the social value of women's unpaid domestic work to the workers' (not capitalist) state. And Claudia Jones presumed such an integral connection by linking the racist segregation of the labour market to the paid and unpaid social reproductive labour of black women.

These are important, but sporadic and incomplete extensions of the social reproduction feminism trajectory. For the most part, the socialist movement adopted the tradition sanctioned by Engels and Bebel— rehearsing and elaborating upon the historical co-emergence of women's oppression and capitalism and urging women to enter waged work, tying (and often subsuming) women's liberation to workplace-based organizations. Certainly, that was the Communist Party USA position.[3] In fact, the CPUSA leadership was openly hostile to challenges to what had become party orthodoxy—as was evident in its sharp rebuke of Jones' white comrade, Mary (Ida May) Inman. Inman, writes one historian, developed "the era's most radical analysis of women's domestic labor."[4] Whereas the CPUSA asserted an internal connection between patriarchy and capitalism, Inman set about to explain it. In so doing, she advanced the first sustained attempt since Wheeler's and Thompson's *Appeal* to subject unpaid domestic labour to a critical political-economic analysis.

IN MARY INMAN'S DEFENSE: THE CPUSA AND SOCIAL REPRODUCTION FEMINISM

In 1910, 16-year-old Inman joined the Oklahoma branch of the Socialist Party of America. By the 1930s she was living in Southern California and active in the CPUSA. There she wrote a series of articles for the party newspaper which formed the basis of her 1940 book, *In Woman's Defense*. Although the book went through three printings in one year, few copies remain of it today.[5] Responding to the CPUSA position, Inman outlines a history of women's labour enriching successive ruling classes. Yet, she quickly moves beyond any simplistic "rule by a class" explanation. Rather, she locates the key to women's oppression in the "very complex" dynamics of capitalist expropriation—specifically in "the relation of housewives' work to social production."[6]

The dynamics are complex, in Inman's view, precisely because they involve much more than exploitation on the shop floor. The broad argument of *In Woman's Defense*—roundly rejected by the party leadership—is that women's work in the home contributes to the production of overall social wealth. Inman calls housewives "the pivot of the system" who provide "indispensable social labour." Because they work in the privacy of their own home, neither housewives nor the wider society sees their connection to the capitalist system, but their labour "is knit into the productive process."[7] To make this point, she compares housewives to cooks in a lumber camp. The camp's owner is the person who ultimately benefits from the cooks' labour, and he would benefit all the more if the cooks were paid nothing at all. The woman at home prepping a factory worker's meals, she observes, similarly benefits the factory owner: "What a sweet arrangement for the capitalists! To have things so fixed that when a woman marries her husband she also marries her work under capitalist production."[8]

Inman positions women's unpaid labour as *productive* work—in both the broad, conventional sense, and in the more technical, Marxist, sense of that term. Directly contradicting the CPUSA's position, she argues that working class women deploy men's (and their own) wages to *produce*, as opposed to simply *consume*, wealth at home. While much work formerly done in the home was now undertaken as waged work (weaving, canning, and schooling, for instance), a woman still maintains her home and raises children. She produces, contends Inman, "the most valuable of all commodities ... Labor Power."[9]

Inman is careful to note that this is not the lot of all women. But it is the lot of "the vast majority of women [who] are without property and have been denied the use of the earth except on the terms of those who claim title to it." The wealthy but dependent woman, she writes, "is a sort of glorified servant ... [who] does no work. There are unglorified servants for that purpose." Similarly, Inman challenges universal biological explanations of women's oppression by emphasizing class distinctions: it is only "subject women" whose labour produces the "subject children" who become the workers and soldiers of tomorrow.[10]

Inman, like other socialists, bemoans the wastefulness of privatized social reproductive work and argues that resources and day nurseries be made available to diminish the drudgery of housework and allow women to more easily work for a wage. But she does not think waged work constitutes a path to freedom. Observing that there are not enough jobs for women in any case, she urges America's 22 million housewives to join "the ranks of socially useful workers" by organizing around "their specific economic needs."[11] That is, she positions the devalued but "socially useful" domestic site of labour as a site of struggle against capital. Proposing that housewives be "given credit" for their work, Inman pictures them taking on such issues as housing and consumer prices, as well as supporting their husbands' trade union struggles.[12]

Thus, for Inman, the struggle against capital need not be limited to the shop floor. It also happens in people's communities. Whereas Kollontai and Zetkin similarly supported community struggles, they did not do so because they thought such actions challenged capital. Rather, in their reckonings, lending support to feminist causes helps build working class unity. According to Inman, however, capital has already unified the working class across gender lines by involving all forms of labour (men's and women's, waged and unwaged) in the process of accumulation. Yet, in depending on the unpaid labour of reproducing workers, capital has also already divided the class along gender lines. That it does both at the same time is why Inman insists that "we take into account the entire *system* of production."[13]

While Inman can be fairly criticized on certain points of theory, the CPUSA leadership cut short any opportunity to debate her ideas.[14] First, party members interrupted a class she taught at the Los Angeles Workers' School to present students the "correct" analysis. Then, the leadership cancelled her class. And finally, a sneering pamphlet by the party's educational director Avram Landy appeared shortly thereafter.[15] In it, Landy accuses Inman of constructing her "theory" (the scare quotes are his) "out of sundry phrases and quotations from Marx, none of which proved anything except her own inability to understand what she reads."[16] He grants that housework is useful, but insists it has no significance in analyzing capitalism. He knows this because Marx and Engels say so:

> The crux of Marx's thesis is that modern industry separates the process of production from the domestic sphere and tends to take the woman into the factory, and though this is accompanied by evils under capitalism, it nevertheless represents the economic foundation for the emancipation of women as well as for a higher form of family.[17]

Motherhood, Landy continues, "is a phenomenon of nature and not of society; it prevails in all social systems." And to the extent that household tasks can be characterized as economic, they are sites of consumption, not production.[18] Despite these and other misguided and naturalist claims, Landy raises some valid questions about Inman's characterization of unpaid domestic work as "productive" (of capitalist value) and of the wage as reflecting the value of women's labour. Yet rather than engage with her ideas, he utterly discounts and disparages them. Not surprisingly, Inman and some of her supporters eventually left the party.

Historians have interpreted this harsh attack as evidence that "CPUSA leaders feared Inman's glorification of housework as holding economic value would support conservative American's goals of forcing women to remain at home."[19] Perhaps. But, as Rebecca Hill points out, this likely lets the party leadership off the hook too easily. It seems just as, if not more, likely that Inman's crime was to have veered from the party line which asserted an abstract working class unity that fails to recognize divisions within it based on social oppression.[20]

THE MYSTIQUE AROUND HOUSEWORK:
FROM FRIEDAN TO BENSTON

Inman's later pamphlet, *The Two Forms of Production under Capitalism*, came out in 1964—the same year another book about housewives topped the country's bestseller lists. Betty Friedan's *The Feminine Mystique*, published a year earlier, had little to do with political economy. Rather, it offered a cultural critique of the myriad ways in which (white, middle class) women are pressured into accepting their fate as keepers of home and hearth.[21]

Ironically, the book appeared on the cusp of the century's most dramatic influx of women—especially married white women with children—into the paid workforce. An expanding post-war economy, increased government investment in schools and other services, higher educational levels among women, and the 1964 Civil Rights Act outlawing ("race-" and gender-based) discriminatory hiring all fueled an unprecedented feminization of the workforce.[22] The numbers of black and Hispanic women workers also jumped as they moved into clerical and sales jobs previously denied them, although the de facto labour market segregation channeled them into low-wage private sector jobs.[23]

Although women gained greater access to the paid workforce, they were hardly equal to men before the law. In the early 1960s, depending upon the state in question, a wife could not claim a right to her husband's property or earnings, drop her divorced husband's name, or open a business in her own name without court approval. She could sue for divorce only if she had proof of repeated instances of adultery (whereas courts required proof of just one instance from the husband). Women also faced discrimination in getting credit or a mortgage and had few to no legal or other recourses if raped, brutalized, or sexually harassed by any man.[24]

The *Feminine Mystique* does not seriously address these societal issues. It focuses on cultural institutions—schools, media, and psychiatry—that perpetuate myths about women's role. And its prognosis is decidedly individualist. Friedan, who earned a BA in Psychology in the 1940s, urges women to "listen to [their] own inner voice to find [their] identity in the changing world." An identity, that is, as a person who earns an income, but not at the cost of her domestic role. Women must create, she writes, "a new life plan, fitting in the love and children and home that have defined femininity in the past with the work toward a greater purpose that shapes the future."[25] The first step in this plan is to reduce time spent on housework by relying on the vacuum cleaner and dishwasher and even, occasionally, instant mashed potatoes. If enough women adopt such a plan, Friedan assures her readers, society will eventually respond by providing the maternity leaves, childcare centers, and other accommodations, reducing barriers to free and equal competition with men on the labour market.

But even Friedan soon realized society might need a little push. So, in 1966, she helped found the National Organization for Women (NOW), penning their Statement of Purpose.[26] Also promoting "partnership" marriages and job retraining for housewives, the Statement reads: "We do not accept the traditional assumption that a woman has to choose between marriage and motherhood, on the one hand, and serious participation in industry or the professions on the other."[27]

Whatever one makes of such advice, it fits fully into the equality feminist framework, treating women's unpaid domestic duties as an obstacle to paid work, and strategizing ways to reduce—if not eliminate—them. And once again, waged labour is held up as the means to independence and emancipation. Only now, along with gaining entry to the labour market, liberal feminists highlighted women's equal treatment within it. Women workers, the Statement notes, tend to be concentrated in poorly paid service sector jobs, and their position had been declining relative to men's. The Statement condemns the "silken curtain of prejudice and discrimination" preventing women from advancing in government, industry, and the professions.

This attention to ameliorating the conditions of women's paid work opens up an important, yet potentially problematic, arena of equality feminism activism. It inspires initiatives such as pay equity and affirmative action hiring. Though these represent concrete advances for many women, they also arguably shift the goal posts. Instead of measuring freedom by the degree of economic independence women enjoy, they measure it by how successful women are *within* the paid labour force, both as wage earners and how far up the management ladder they climb. Since there is only so much room at the top, however, equality feminism (increasingly in the twenty-first century) feeds a "corporate feminist" strategy that promotes the advancement of a few women at the expense of many.[28]

Attention to women's working conditions also provided an avenue for NOW to address the sorts of questions Claudia Jones had raised a quarter of a century earlier. Pointing out that three-quarters of working women are in clerical, factory, and service jobs, the Statement adds, "about two-thirds of Negro women workers are in the lowest paid service occupations." But it develops no analysis of this, except to say a few paragraphs later that "Negro women [are] victims of the double discrimination of race and sex." Notably, Jones' third axis of oppression, class, is absent from this formulation.

Inman similarly failed to adequately theorize the racialized nature of women's work. Written a decade earlier than Jones' articles, *In Woman's Defense* periodically compares women's predicament with that of African Americans and observes a connection between the two struggles.[29] In *The Two Forms of Production Under Capitalism* (1964), Inman notes that "Negro women are particularly victimized by the present system." Though sympathetic, she shows remarkably little analytic interest in the question of race while reinforcing racial stereotypes of black women as poor mothers: "We have seen them cleaning house for somebody else on Saturday when they were already exhausted from a week of such work, yet had to still go home and do their own weekend shopping, cooking and other work, while small children were often endangered by their absence."[30] The inability to engage with issues of racism on a theoretical level is all the more surprising and disappointing given that, in the 1960s, a broad-based movement of black and Hispanic welfare and civil rights feminists consistently and vigorously drew attention to racism's integral relation to issues of class and gender experienced by working class mothers.[31]

Inman's 1964 publication is a short, self-published pamphlet circulated primarily among a small west-coast circle of feminists. Only five years later, however, a broadly similar argument appearing in the Marxist journal, *Monthly Review*, would capture the imagination of a far larger audience. Its author was Margaret Benston, "a feminist, a marxist, a musician and a political activist" who at the time was a professor of Chemistry at Simon Fraser University in Canada.[32] Benston does not appear to have read Inman, but her 1969 article, "The Political Economy of Women's Liberation," advances Inman's views that women's unpaid work in the home constitutes production (not consumption) essential to the capitalist process of value creation.[33]

Unlike Inman, however, Benston stresses that housewives do not engage in capitalistically "productive" labour because they do not produce *for* the market. Housewives create use values, she observes, not exchange values: their "products" are consumed immediately in the privacy of their homes by people with whom they share family ties. Such work, she then suggests, is pre-capitalist:

> [The] household ... constitutes an individual production unit, a pre-industrial entity, in the same way that peasant farmers or cottage weavers constitute pre-industrial production units. The main features are clear with the reduplicative, kin-based, private nature of the work being the most important.[34]

Despite its noncapitalist nature, Benston insists, housework "is very profitable to those who own the means of production." It lowers the overall cost of production because a single wage covers the cost of two people's "socially necessary" labour, and it institutionalizes in the figure of the housewife a highly flexible reserve army of labour, whose low wages fuel competition among workers and thereby lowering wages in general.[35] Moreover, she suggests that the private family arrangement creates some level of social stability because, with children and a wife reliant on the wage, a husband is less likely to strike, change jobs, or forego work all together. Benston's position here differs from critical equality feminism which claims unpaid domestic labour is outside *and irrelevant to* capital.

Although Benston identifies "the material basis" of women's oppression as the fact that women are excluded from "the money economy" in a society in which money measures value, hers is not an argument about women's dependence upon men. Rather, she insists that the structural relationship of women's unpaid work to paid work is the critical lever of oppression, and thus of liberation. Equality in paid work, writes Benston, is an important goal. But it will not liberate women: "As long as housework and childcare remain a matter of private production and the responsibility of women, wage-earning women will simply carry a double work-load."[36] She argues for the socialization of such work but cautions that only a socialist system will put human welfare above profit; in capitalist societies, socialization of care work is likely to dehumanize women, not liberate them.

For Benston then the promise of women's liberation does not lie in expanding government services such as childcare and healthcare, however much those are important aspects of the struggle. It lies in women asserting control over the conditions in which they perform unpaid work. Like Inman, Benston calls on housewives to assert pressure—not for waged work in the first instance, but against their "exploitation" in the home. It is because housewives play a necessary role in the creation of profit that their community-based actions are part of the struggle against capital. Such actions, she argues, "impede the functioning of the family" while also counteracting the tendency for capitalists to treat women as a reserve army of labour.[37] Housewives, in other words, have a role to play in the transition to socialism *because of (not despite)* their unique position relative to capital.

THEORIZING PATRIARCHY AND CAPITALISM

While many on the Marxist left and in the Civil Rights movement did not take Benston and her interlocutors seriously, they were unable to silence them as the CPUSA had silenced Inman. Indeed, for the first time, an international activist layer of socialist feminists began engaging with a political-economic critique of women's unpaid domestic work.[38] The Domestic Labour Debate (as that engagement came to be called) challenged and built upon Benston's specific formulations about the relationship between unpaid and paid work. Its contributors aimed to solve the riddle of exactly how women's unpaid labour in the home is part of the process of creating surplus value. They aimed, that is, to clearly identify the material basis of women's oppression and thereby identify *who*—capitalists, men, or capitalists *and* men—had an interest in subjugating women.[39]

Radical feminists, however, posed that question most sharply. 1969 was also the year another article about women's domestic labour circulated widely: "The Politics of Housework" by New York Redstockings feminist Pat Mainardi. In an imagined dialogue with her husband, who she says was "too hip" to turn down her proposal that they split housework, Mainardi raises and then counters numerous excuses men use to get out of doing their share. She concludes in the man's voice: "Oppression is built into this System. I, as the white American male, receive the benefits of this System. I don't want to give them up."[40]

The "system" here is not capitalism, but patriarchy. Kate Millett's book, *Sexual Politics*, claiming that patriarchy was the fundamental power dynamic of all societies, past and present, had also appeared in 1969. And before long, many radical feminists were using Marxist language to explain how patriarchy constitutes a system in its own right, distinct from capitalism. For example, Hodee Edwards, a CPUSA contemporary of Inman's who also left the party, wrote in 1971:

> Women as a class (irrespective of other classes they may also belong to as workers, middle class women and so on) have as their main task in our society ... the production of labor power ... The man also—in all but name—owns the "means of production" of "his commodity," namely the individual woman.[41]

Hodee and other radical feminists may have drawn on political-economic concepts, but they understood the relation between the two systems as parallel: capitalism and patriarchy mirrored each other in certain ways but operated according to distinct dynamics and bases of power. Even if they were often critical of capitalism, they attributed women's oppression to the patriarchal system, which revolved around the unpaid work women did for men.

Socialist feminists, however, continued to grapple with resolving the relational question, now increasingly posed as a problem of two *systems*, capitalism and patriarchy. It's not possible to recount the full scope and significance of their efforts. Instead, I focus on two influential, related but distinct, directions in which social reproduction feminism develops in the 1970s. These directions are evident in the international Wages for Housework initiative, on the one hand, and *Woman's Consciousness, Man's World*, written in 1973 by UK socialist feminist Sheila Rowbotham, on the other.

Wages for Housework

In 1972, Mariarosa Dalla Costa, Silvia Federici, Brigitte Galtier, and Selma James—representing feminist organizations in Italy, the United States, France, and England, respectively—founded the International Feminist Collective which then launched Wages for Housework (WfH) campaigns in Padua and London. Over the next five years, feminists in multiple North American and European cities, as well as in Trinidad & Tobago followed suit. Although the campaign spawned more critics than adherents within the women's movement, "one might say, without exaggerating, that [it] affected all of militant feminism in the 1970s in North America and Europe to some degree."[42]

The leading WfH theorists (Federici, Dalla Costa, and James) distinguished their perspective from conventional socialist feminism by stressing the significance of patriarchal oppression as an axis of power. As Federici explains in her 1975 pamphlet, *Wages Against Housework*, capital *and men* both benefit from women's oppression:

> In the same way as god created Eve to give pleasure to Adam, so did capital create the housewife to service the male worker physically, emotionally and sexually, to raise his children, mend his socks, patch up his ego when it is crushed by the work and the social relations ... that capital has reserved for him.[43]

In insisting that men too have an interest in sustaining women's oppression, WfH feminists added a layer of complexity to socialist feminist theories that tended to stress capital's interests above all else. At the same time, they inspired a reconceptualization of capitalism itself. Capitalism, they proposed, is not simply an *economic* system of "free" waged labour; it is also, at its heart—in the creation of the very labour power it requires to produce the profits on which it thrives—a *political* system of *unfreedom*.[44] And in response to radical feminists, WfH feminists argued that rather than two distinct systems, one economic in nature, the other political, capitalism and patriarchy are reciprocal constituent parts of a thing that is better termed *patriarchal capitalism*.

WfH feminists therefore proposed that women organize separately from men, while also making their demand on capital (through the state) for wages. They did not, however, advance the wage demand as an end in itself. They did not simply advocate, that is, for women's economic independence. Rather, the campaign tied its demand to a broader political goal. Wages for housework is "only a basis, a perspective, from which to start," explain Dalla Costa and James. Its "merit is to link immediately female oppression, subordination and isolation to their material foundation: female exploitation."[45] As such, the demand that housewives be given a wage reveals the power women have to withdraw from housework, to *refuse* it, in the same way that striking waged workers stand up to capital.[46]

It is helpful to cite Federici's elaboration of this point at length because it illustrates just how convoluted the thinking behind the WfH campaign was—and therefore just how questionable it was as a mobilizing strategy. According to Federici:

When we struggle for wages for housework we struggle unambig-uously and directly against our social role … we do not struggle to enter capitalist relations, because we have never been out of them. We struggle to break capital's plan for women … [Ours] is a revolutionary demand not because by itself it destroys capital, but because it forces capital to restructure social relations in terms more favorable to us and consequently more favorable to the unity of the class. In fact, to demand wages for housework does not mean to say that if we are paid we will continue to do this work. It means precisely the opposite. To say that we want wages for housework is the first step towards refusing to do it, because the demand for a wage makes our work visible, which is the most indispensable condition to begin to struggle against it …

Wages for housework is only the beginning, but its message is clear from now on, they have to pay us because as women we do not guarantee anything any longer … We are housemaids, prostitutes, nurses, shrinks … From now on we want money for each moment of it, so that we can refuse some of it and eventually all of it.[47]

The campaign's revolutionary impulse of refusal translated poorly on the ground. The women's movement—both supporters and detractors of WfH within it—tended to focus on the wage goal as a more straightfor-ward demand for money. And critics condemned that focus as narrow, reformist, and potentially damaging for women. They argued, among other things, that it turns the state into housewives' employers, thereby granting it the right to regulate women's lives more closely (imagine home inspections to ensure the kids are properly fed) while releasing governments (and capitalists) from the responsibility to provide essen-tial social services in the community. As Louise Toupin observes, "When it is reduced to a monetary demand, the entire political analysis with which [WfH] was associated, as well as its subversive capacity, is too easily bypassed."[48]

Sheila Rowbotham

Sheila Rowbotham published three books in the early 1970s: *Women, Resistance and Revolution* (1972), *Hidden from History* (1973), and *Woman's Consciousness, Man's World* (1973). She went on to publish many more, but these were the books that forged modern socialist feminist politics in the United Kingdom and had a huge impact beyond British borders as well. More than a century after Anna Wheeler and

William Thompson had subjected women's unpaid labour to political economic critique, Rowbotham—"one of Britain's most important ... feminist thinkers"—managed to get Britons to seriously engage with a social reproduction feminist perspective.[49]

In contrast to the WfH theorists, Rowbotham agreed with Benston that women's unpaid work in the home constitutes a distinct (noncapitalist) mode of production. It differs from industrial production, she suggests, because it is oriented to meeting family members' needs (not capital's need for profit) and because "social relations within the *family mode of production* are not directly on the cash-nexus."[50] This distinct set of social relations explains why women develop a unique consciousness, one attuned to the values of preserving families. It also means that pre-capitalist relations of domination live on in new forms within the family. Because marriage is a contract based on a prior inequality of social power that upholds the remnants of a patriarchal system, men continue to dominate women—despite and against those capitalist tendencies to treat all people, men and women, black and white, as equally exploitable labourers.

Rowbotham conceptualizes the family mode of production as separate from but subordinate to the capitalist mode of production. It is subordinate in the sense that capitalism mandates the division between production and reproduction in the first place as a means of ensuring an ongoing supply of labour power at minimal cost. But the family is also its own basis of social power. Women—their bodies and their labour—are men's "property," and men exercise and maintain their power by appropriating the use values women produce in the household. As a result, Rowbotham proposes, "Not only does women's labour maintain a subordinate mode of production within capitalism, but women are generally subordinate to men as group within capitalist society."[51]

Yet there is a flip side to these familial power relations. As a separate mode of production, the family is not simply responsive to the needs of capital. It influences capitalism through its regulation of the production of labour power. The family can serve "to restrict [capital's] expansion" as when mothers' household duties keep them off the labour market or when protective legislation and compulsory education pre-empt the exploitation of young children. Ultimately, writes Rowbotham:

The family is both essential for capital's reproduction, and a brake on its use of human labour power. The values of the family are both rational for the maintenance of the inhuman relations of commodity production, and irrational for a system of organising the reproduction of human labour which is completely designed to produce commodities efficiently and has freed itself from all earlier property relations.[52]

Coming back time and again to the contradiction at the heart of capitalism, Rowbotham sees in it an opening for women and for the working class:

Women's liberation has been formed by the conflicting pressure of these antagonisms upon the life and social relations of women. This means we have a unique opportunity of attacking the consequences of capitalist society not only at the point of production, but also at the point of procreation.[53]

Rowbotham calls for feminists to define their own issues while also linking their struggle to that of the class more generally.[54] Limiting their goals to demands such as equal pay will not be enough. "Beyond just asking for more, if we are ever to end the spiraling whirlwind of simply economic inroads into the structure of capitalist society ... we need to develop notions of what an alternative society would be like." The socialist left needs to learn from "female consciousness [which] will continue to reflect the features inherent in female production in the family."[55]

To the extent that women's unpaid work occurs *outside* capitalism, Rowbotham insists, women hold the secret to creating an alternative, better, society. Yet, because it is also—at the same time—*inside* capitalism, feminist goals need to be incorporated into the wider class struggle. Socialists need to find "the means of translating the experience of one group to another without merely annexing the weaker to the stronger." They need, in other words, a pluralistic organization that can both recognize the specificity of oppression *and* the generality of capital: "It is not just groups which have a position of power at the point of production in the advanced sectors of the capitalist economy, but the organization of groups whose consciousness spans several dimensions of oppression which becomes crucial in a revolutionary movement."[56]

TAKING STOCK: THE TROUBLE WITH HOUSEWORK

The WfH campaign and Rowbotham's early books theorize women's unpaid domestic labour in different ways. For the WfH theorists, housework and childcare constitute a necessary and *direct* contribution to capitalist value production. For Rowbotham, they are a necessary and *indirect* contribution. That distinction undergirds two related but specific strategic orientations. Still, the WfH and Rowbotham positions have much in common. Taking stock of what they share reveals certain key strengths and weaknesses of this era's social reproduction feminism.

To begin with its strengths: Benston, the WfH theorists, and Rowbotham all highlight capitalism's dependence upon *"extra-economic"* (or *socio-political*) forms of power.[57] That is, they show how capitalism cannot be fully understood in terms of the production and exchange of commodities alone. Rather, capital draws into its orbit other social relations, with distinct values and logics, shaping them to meet its unquenchable thirst for profit while also contending with the ways in which these other sets of relations may obstruct the realization of its goals.

In making this argument, social reproduction feminists take issue with the socialist left's narrow focus on waged labour. They particularly challenge its tendency to attribute to capitalism a unilateral drive toward the equalization of labour.[58] Certainly, waged labour is elemental to capitalist accumulation as the source of the temporally quantifiable substance of exchange value that produces capital. And such labour is abstracted from its variable, concrete, useful properties and treated as an interchangeable expenditure of brains, muscles, and nerves measurable in hours and minutes. Yet, as Marx well knew, capitalist labour is a two-sided thing: it is both abstract and concrete. And in insisting upon a broad definition of labour, social reproduction feminism recenters the concreteness (most specifically in this era, the gendering) of labouring bodies in analysis and politics, calling attention to the fundamental contradiction of capitalism: the fact that "capital's drive to fully subsume labour, to instrumentalise it, to strip it of all embodiment and subjectivity, runs up against its dependence on concrete, living labour—sentient, embodied, thinking, self-conscious labour."[59]

Rather than treat capitalism as a theoretical or abstract economic (self-enclosed) *system*, Benston, Rowbotham, and the WfH theorists develop an analytic framework which insists upon investigating the concrete, embodied, nature of actually existing socio-historical relations. It is a framework which makes it possible to conceptualize and explore the logic behind capital's interaction with social power relations such as patriarchy. The very term *patriarchal capitalism* conveys this much: neither patriarchy nor capitalism constitute wholly discrete realms, but neither does one collapse into the other. They are "mutually" or "co-constitutive," to use a term associated with intersectionality feminism. And, significantly, that mutuality contains the irresolvable contradiction of life against capital.

The potential of social reproduction feminism to reorient Marxist theorizing, however, was only partially evident in the 1970s. It is glimpsed in the insistence that capitalism relies on both economic and "extra-economic" forms of social oppression, as well as in the insistence that the processes of life-making can act as a "brake" on the drive to accumulation and dispossession. But these analyses also share a key weakness: they focus too narrowly on unpaid housework and childcare as "the pivot" (to use Inman's term) of the system. In so doing, they introduce theoretical oversights and ambiguities that simply cannot be sustained in the face of empirical evidence. For instance, the WfH theorists grant housework undue leverage by positioning it as a common denominator of women's oppression. *All* women (working class, bourgeois, black, white, peasant, colonized) are oppressed by virtue of their status as potential and actual unpaid reproducers of labour power: "All women, in fact, as we well know, are fundamentally 'housewives,' that is 'workers in the home,' for housework is the first and only front where we all are and which determines all aspects of our life."[60]

Rowbotham does not make the same claim, but she so tightly maps gender to the distinction between paid and unpaid labour that she ends up universalizing women's experience in a similar way. Despite acknowledging that women participate in the workforce, Rowbotham stresses that their "main responsibility is still the home ... [in which] the woman essentially serves the man in exchange for care and protection." Housework is thus an unambiguous signifier of womanhood, one that comprises their shared experience of oppression—a perspective that leads Rowbotham to make baldly false statements such as: "Work in capitalism is something men do. Men are the providers because they are paid money. Women are only allowed money by their husbands."[61]

These strong claims for the determinative impact of housework on women's lives can too easily be understood as attributing women's oppression to the gender division of labour itself, and not to its structural relation to the processes of capitalist value production. That is, in emphasizing the (unpaid, subservient) nature of the unpaid work women do as the basis of women's oppression, they lose sight of the social reproduction feminism insight grounding oppression in the contradictory relation between paid and unpaid work. As a result, they reinforce the idea that social reproduction feminism is a white woman's feminism.

Angela Davis takes Inman, Benston, and the WfH campaign to task precisely for their failure to account for black feminist insights about racism's role in shaping women's lives. She points out that the full-time housewife has only ever "reflected a partial reality ... rooted in the social conditions of the bourgeoisie and middle classes." Paying housewives a wage is no solution as immigrant and black women in the United States "have been receiving wages for housework for untold decades" as paid domestic servants in white women's homes.[62] Davis goes on to contrast black and white women's unpaid housework, picking up on Claudia Jones' observation that, for many black women who endured slavery and its legacy, housework was the space in which they exercised a measure of control. Chandra Mohanty follows Davis with a similarly trenchant critique. Mohanty objects to the ways in which this era's social reproduction feminists universalized white Western women's experiences. Insisting on the need for a more concrete, culturally variable, concept of patriarchy, she questions whether *any* comprehensive theory of social relations was possible.[63]

These criticisms identify something more than the racialized thinking or theoretical oversights. They identify a theoretical obfuscation, a tension pervading 1970s social reproduction feminism. Despite historicizing patriarchy by emphasizing that women's oppression is rooted in the work women do to reproduce labour power specifically for capital, the WfH and Rowbotham contributions discussed here simultaneously *dehistoricize* patriarchy by granting it an undefended universalism. For instance, even though Rowbotham argues that patriarchy is a sort of lesser power, existing within a world governed ultimately by capital and in contradiction to the erstwhile equalizing dynamics of capitalism, she identifies patriarchy with the *family mode of production*—a set of relations that are sustained through a power dynamic based on gender difference. Men, by virtue of their gender, exercise power over women through their "ownership" or control of women's bodies and labours. This conception of patriarchy is difficult to distinguish from the radical feminism position outlined above and suggests a dualistic conception of power relations in which patriarchy is a system unto itself, operating alongside and in conjunction with but ultimately at the behest of the capitalist system.

The WfH theorists give less ground in this regard. While insisting that unpaid housework is the common denominator of all women's lives and therefore the lever of patriarchal power, they more pointedly emphasize its capitalist imperative. According to Federici and Nicole Cox, "Far from being a precapitalist structure, the family, as we know it in the 'West,' is a creation of capital for capital, as an institution that is supposed to guarantee the quantity and quality of labor power and its control."[64] But this leads to an opposite, equally untenable, position: it dissolves women's oppression into the economic logic of capitalist accumulation and dispossession. Patriarchy here becomes a function of class exploitation, something that capitalism calls into being and molds according to its overriding drive to create value.

This same functionalism creeps into WfH theorization of racism. Contrary to Davis' critique of the campaign, James made racialized paid domestic work central to the UK Wages for Housework Committee political activism from the beginning. Acknowledging the deep significance of divisions among women, James comments that although women "share overwork and poverty … race, immigration and other divides determine what kind of work we do, how much we do, under what circumstances and for what returns."[65] But when it comes to explaining why and how racism interacts with capital, James offers a functionalist (and circular) explanation: "The labour that capital wants done is divided and each category parceled out internationally as the life work, the destiny, the identity of specific sets of workers." That is, an international division of labour (itself a product of capitalist imperialism) reinforces racism by funneling conquered peoples (and women) into low-wage work. This "hierarchy of labour powers" captures something descriptively true about capitalism, but as an explanation, it simply collapses the logic of racism into the logic of capitalist accumulation.[66]

CONCLUSION

In granting such determinative weight to housework, 1970s social reproduction feminism confounds its theoretical premises. It identifies both the structural relation of unpaid labour to paid labour *and* the nature of unpaid gendered labour as the material basis of women's oppression in capitalism. Insofar as it locates that basis in the latter, however, this era's social reproduction feminism undermines its commitment to an integrated analysis of patriarchal capitalism. Instead, it defaults to a critical equality feminist position, and the attendant problems of dual systems or class reductionism.[67] These equally problematic analytic frameworks led Heidi Hartmann to conclude in 1979 that Marxism and feminism are partners in an "unhappy marriage."

By the early 1980s, social reproduction feminism—and with it, Marxist feminism—appeared to have run its course. Many of its critics had lost faith in materialist theories, reflecting and fueling a shift away from class analysis that mirrored the political defeat of the working class and civil rights movements on the ground as neoliberal governments came to power in country after country. Most socialist feminists began shifting their attention from women's labour to cultural, discursive, explanations of women's oppression—abandoning attempts to think through a more complex socio-materialist understanding of oppression in capitalist societies.[68]

But there were some holdouts. Black feminism, developing as a distinct theoretical orientation in the 1970s, pushed back against the tendency to abandon the material world while continuing to insist upon and develop theories that accounted for more complexly integrated experiences of women's oppression. At the same time, pockets of socialist feminists continued to explore the world from within a social reproduction feminism paradigm, albeit paying only scant attention to their critics for the most part. That, however, has changed in the last couple of decades. Today, social reproduction feminism is in the process of renewal once again. Only this time, it is more seriously engaging with issues of racism and other social oppressions. As the next chapter argues, this renewal crucially involves decentering housework from its theoretical apparatus and foregrounding the contradiction posed to capital by the reproduction of life, whatever social relations are involved in that reproduction.

7
Renewing Social Reproduction Feminism

Our history knows no category called "women's work": there is "white men's" work, "white women's" work, and "n[.....] work." "N[.....] work" has its roots in slavery in the "new world", and in the inscriptions of less-than-human characteristics to Black peoples as a whole.
—Dionne Brand, 1993

The above passage by novelist, poet, and activist Dionne Brand is at once evocative and provocative.[1] Tying the dehumanizing nature of racism to the distinct histories of black people, it implicitly critiques all preceding feminism that writes black women's experiences out of its accounts of women's labour. And it stresses the particularity of experiences, black's and white's, men's and women's—while at the same time gesturing to a shared world in which everyone labours.

Many white socialist feminists worked politically with anti-racist activists in the 1960s and after, partially engaging with their critique. Nonetheless, they largely remained committed to a conception of the world and a theoretical orientation that could not accommodate black feminist concerns. That is, they proved unable or unwilling to think through how the complexity black feminism introduces to the concept of domestic labour challenges the socialist feminist positioning of that concept in explanations of patriarchal capitalism.

Black feminists had repeatedly pointed out that not all housework is unpaid and not all women see the work they do to maintain their households (and communities) as inherently oppressive. They also insisted that women are oppressed in ways that have nothing to do with housework. Clearly, then, unpaid housework must be abandoned as the universalizing category on which the explanation of women's oppression pivots.[2] And if it is, what is left of the socialist feminist perspective? Not much, concluded many. In certain respects, they were correct: because critical equality feminism identifies the unpaid and isolating nature of domestic work as *the key problem* to be resolved, decentering housework from its analysis does indeed leave little to discuss.

Social reproduction feminism, on the other hand, is not so restricted. It in fact offers theoretical space to develop a more complex, integrative analysis—although such a task involves resolving the theoretical ambiguities and tensions outlined in the previous chapter. This is accomplished, first, by unhinging the understanding of social reproductive labour from an ahistorical and universal concept of housework; and second, by emphasizing and developing the insight about the *relation* of capitalistically "productive" to "unproductive" work. It further involves doing the necessary empirical and theoretical work to consider how that relation is structured not just by sexism, but by social oppressions in general, from racism and heterosexism to settler colonialism, ableism and beyond.

This chapter explores the contours of that theoretical space. It begins with a short discussion of those who directly called for it, the Combahee River Collective. I then review Lise Vogel's formulation of social reproduction feminism that expands and elaborates that space—showing how it sets the stage for subsequent socialist feminists to move well beyond the limitations of earlier social reproduction feminism. Vogel's coherent and insightful political-economic analysis situating women's work within capitalist relations of production dislodges unpaid housework from its place as the conceptual heart of socialist feminist analysis, thereby undercutting tendencies toward theoretical dualism and class reductionism. Critically building on Vogel's analysis, socialist feminists today are putting resistance to oppression *and* exploitation at the center of the class struggle—efforts I explore in Chapter 8.

"WHITE WOMAN LISTEN!" BLACK FEMINISM AND THE COMPLEXITY OF OPPRESSION

In the summer of 1974, a group of black, lesbian, socialist feminists began meeting regularly in Boston. Alternately inspired by and critical of the black feminist, black power and (white-dominated) socialist and anti-war groups prominent in the civil rights struggle with whom they had been organizing, the women formed the Combahee River Collective.[3] According to CRC co-founder Barbara Smith, the collective aimed "first of all … to make a political place for people like ourselves." A place, that is, where they could speak about, reflect upon, and organize against their experiences of sexism, racism, homophobia, *and* class exploitation.

As another co-founder, Dimita Frazier, points out, "We in ourselves, in our very bodies represented another sort of emerging understanding of the complexity of politics."[4]

Thus, while white socialist feminists were sorting through political-economic questions of value and domestic labour, the CRC was also rethinking Marxism. But its members were asking a different set of questions. In April 1977, Frazier, Barbara Smith, and Beverly Smith shared the Combahee River Collective Statement, which they had developed from ideas circulating with broader CRC discussions.[5] Avtar Brah calls the CRC Statement:

> one of the most powerful documents of women of color feminism—indeed, of all categories of feminism … widely acknowledged as a forerunner to our current debates on intersectionality … and prefigur[ing] later debates on how to theorize questions of "embodiment" and "experience."[6]

Although the CRC's class politics are sometimes overlooked, the Statement is a singularly coherent articulation of the need for a *socialist* feminist analysis of multiple, "interlocking" oppressions. Barbara Smith stresses this in an interview with Keeanga-Yamahtta Taylor, noting the significance of the group's interactions with socialists who at least had an analysis (however imperfect) of class and race. Smith observes that "anti-capitalism is what gives [the CRC Statement] the sharpness, the edge, the thoroughness, the revolutionary potential."[7]

That critical edge is embedded in a call for a distinctive approach to theory and practice—one that addresses both the particular and shared experiences of oppressed people. Referring to the "manifold and simultaneous oppressions that all women of color face," the authors insist that "our liberation is a necessity not … an adjunct to somebody else's." At the same time, black women are seen as part of a larger struggle, "the liberation of all oppressed peoples," which requires destroying capitalism, imperialism, and patriarchy:

> The most general statement of our politics at the present time would be that we are actively committed to struggling against racial, sexual, heterosexual, and class oppression, *and see as our particular task the development of integrated analysis and practice based upon the fact that the major systems of oppression are interlocking.*[8]

Or, as Beverly Smith quipped in an interview with Taylor, "No, it is not as simple-minded and flat and one-dimensional as you all may think it is."[9]

The gist of the CRC Statement was not new. Black feminists had, as Chapter 5 makes clear, been pointing out the multi-dimensionality of oppression and complexity of politics for a long time. Not only had they consistently stressed black women's "double" and "triple" oppressions, Maria Stewart, Anna Julia Cooper, Sadie Alexander, Claudia Jones, and others had also located that complexity within white feminism's central analytic category, domestic labour. Recall, for example, Stewart's "fair daughters of Africa" denied advancement because they are condemned to scrub "iron pots and kettles."[10] Or Jones' call to end the government's "shunt[ing of] Negro women, despite their qualifications" into low-waged domestic work.[11] And, in the post-war decades, black, Hispanic, and immigrant women pushing for welfare reform also drew attention to the complexities of unpaid domestic work.

Nor was the CRC the only black feminist voice in the 1970s driving home these points. Women in the civil rights struggle had regularly called out the sexism of fellow organizers in the Student Nonviolent Coordinating Committee, the Black Panthers, and other organizations.[12] Among them was Communist Party USA member and Black Panther supporter Angela Davis.[13] Davis is of interest here because her 1981 book, *Women, Race, and Class*, advances the CRC call for an integrated analysis in a direction compatible with social reproduction feminism—even as she mounts a powerful critique of some within that tradition for their narrow focus on housework. To begin, Davis rejects the premise of the Wages for Housework campaign that housewives are the "secret worker[s] inside the capitalist production process." Citing an editorial from a CPUSA periodical to support her analysis, she insists that housework is a "prerequisite" for the regeneration of labour power.[14]

At the same time, Davis complicates any social reproduction framework that narrowly focuses on housework. She points to the example of South Africa, where the regime has deliberately undermined black domestic life. And like Claudia Jones before her, she emphasizes that most black women have worked outside the house, with one-third of them, in 1960, working as paid domestics, mostly in white people's homes.[15] Throughout the book Davis moves between analyses of black women's racialized waged and unwaged work, treating racism, sexism, and class exploitation as systemically related—foregrounding, as David

McNally notes, "the interplay of the production of value and the reproduction of human beings."[16]

Despite these powerful critiques, most white socialist feminists just didn't seem to get it. While some supported anti-racist struggles, they were less inclined to fully engage with black feminist *analysis*. That is, they did not consider the black feminist critique as reason to rethink the premises of their gender analysis.[17] Many continued to (implicitly or explicitly) position unpaid housework as a pivotal and universal category of their analysis and, in so doing, either wrote black women out of their feminism or treated racism as a secondary form of oppression, external to the workings of patriarchal capitalism. No wonder that by 1982 Hazel Carby, author of the widely read and aptly titled article, "White Woman Listen!" observed, "it is as if we didn't exist."[18]

In the meantime, black feminists began deepening and extending their conceptual apparatus in ways that better fit their worlds. Building on the CRC Statement's discussion of "interlocking oppressions," many began developing a more robust intersectionality feminist framework, one that seemed capable of articulating the particularity of experience without losing sight of its complexity.[19] I have addressed the strengths and limits of intersectionality feminism elsewhere. What interests me at this point is how that approach's insights and commitments are critically appropriated in the current renewal of social reproduction feminism.[20]

That renewal is premised on dislodging unpaid housework as the privileged category determining women's fate in capitalism, and it begins with Lise Vogel's 1983 book, *Marxism and the Oppression of Women: Toward a Unitary Theory*. Rather than analyzing household relations of unpaid work, Vogel stresses the meaning of the necessary-but-contradictory relation between social reproductive labour and the processes of capital accumulation. Others before her had identified this relational dynamic. But they tended to confuse matters by framing the discussion of women's oppression exclusively in terms of patriarchal relations within the household. Vogel pushes back against that tendency. For Vogel, there is no singular cause of women's oppression. Rather, there is a systemic logic that sets the conditions whereby people reproduce themselves, on the one hand, and capital produces value, on the other. And women's oppression is sustained and shaped in the working through of the dynamics of that relationship.

Here Vogel lays the necessary groundwork for socialist feminism to develop a robust politics of class solidarity. Rather than calling unpaid housewives the revolutionary feminist subject, her approach allows for an expanded and diverse array of potential class subjects: all those who work to (re)produce the lives of workers—whether their labour is paid or unpaid, whether they do so within households, in state institutions, or as community organizers. Social reproductive labour here is then broadly defined. It includes the daily and generational work women have typically performed of giving birth to and raising and caring for children. But it also includes the work people do to sustain themselves and others as human beings more generally, their individual and collective "survival strategies through which people accomplish their basic life tasks."[21] While on a fundamental level, the goal of social reproductive labour is to support life, it is at the same time a means of ensuring adequate supplies of labour power are available to support capital.

And rather than seek to understand oppression exclusively in terms of the wagelessness, isolation, or other hardships of women's housework, this perspective calls for a broad exploration of the mechanisms and social relations involved in the devaluation of life-making. Gender relations are certainly part of that devaluation—although they can and will take many different forms including, but not limited to, private patriarchal households in which women perform the bulk of the unpaid labour. So too, however, are other social oppressions (such as the racist relations that facilitated the reproduction of black South African workers in the Apartheid era that Davis mentions or the heterosexism and transphobic dynamics that marginalize and threaten the life-making activities of queer and gender nonconforming people). While Vogel does not explore the multiplicity of dynamics that are potentially in play, many who draw on her work have begun to do the theoretical and empirical work that reveals how the devaluing and dehumanization of life necessary to capital is entangled with racist, heterosexist, settler colonial, and other oppressive relations.

BEYOND HOUSEWORK: TOWARD AN INTEGRATIVE THEORY

Instead of directly engaging with the theoretical challenges posed by black feminism, those developing social reproduction feminism were more inclined to respond to critics citing its class reductionism and/or theoretical dualism. As a result, we see some important attempts to develop a "unitary" theory of gender and class from socialist feminists Pat and Hugh Armstrong, Johanna Brenner and Maria Ramas, Martha

Gimenez, Wally Seccombe, Iris Young and Eli Zaretsky, to name a few.[22] Vogel's *Marxism and the Oppression of Women* similarly claims to elaborate a unitary theory but stands out from these other contributions for its more thorough-going re-theorization of Marx's critique of capital.

Vogel revisits Marx's theory of capitalist relations of production, focusing on the socio-historic dynamics that drive the production of labour power—the one "special commodity" whose production Marx never rigorously examines.[23] Others before Vogel had also reconceptualized capitalism as a political system of unfreedom but they had not focused as Vogel does on *the systemic logic* that informs capital's reliance on oppressive relations. And, as I argue in Chapter 6, their ultimate insistence that unpaid housework constitutes the basis of all women's oppression clashed with and ultimately undermined the coherence of their perspective—leaving them open to charges that they advanced either a dual systems or class reductionist outlook.

Vogel's analysis is free of this problem. Like others before her, she argues that labour power is produced and reproduced (primarily) within the family, which is structured internally through social relations based on age and gender difference. But rather than make the family's internal structure and dynamics the focus of her investigation, she examines the nature of the interaction between it and capital. That is, the subject of her investigation is not the patriarchal household. It is the socio-historic logic through which capitalism and the patriarchal household are co-constituted.

Therein Vogel identifies and unpacks a deep and abiding contradiction. Capitalists do not directly control the (re)production of labour power (the processes of which involve, she insists, capitalistically "unproductive" labour).[24] They do, however, pay the wages and some of the taxes through which workers gain the means of subsistence to reproduce themselves. Because competition compels capitalists to keep wages and taxes as low as possible, the social reproduction of labour presents them with a dilemma: they require human labour power but must constrain the conditions of life that generate it. As Vogel observes, "From the point of view of capital, the social reproduction of the workforce is simultaneously indispensable and an obstacle to accumulation."[25] *Capitalism thus exists only by consistently thwarting the flourishing of human life on which it nonetheless depends.*

Ruling classes resolve this dilemma in different ways, but the historically dominant resolution has been through off-loading as much responsibility for the reproduction of labour power on private households as possible. And because women's biologically given capacities for childbirth and breastfeeding are critical to the success of that strategy, they have since the dawn of capitalism facilitated those relations, processes, and institutions that both encourage and control women's reproductive labour (both as breeders and caretakers)—while also keeping the costs of so doing as low as possible. Thus, for Vogel, "women's oppression in class societies is rooted in *their differential position* with respect to generational replacement processes"—and not in the processes of unpaid housework and childcare themselves.[26]

As far back as the 1820s, William Thompson and Anna Wheeler observed that the production of life was part and parcel of the production of social wealth. And in the following century, theorists from Inman to Benston to Dalla Costa analyzed ways in which that relation drew specific patriarchal relations into the very constitution of capitalist wealth. Vogel provides the most coherent theory of that reciprocal constitution by unpacking the political-economic logic which grounds women's oppression in the capitalist relations of production themselves. In so doing, she reveals the conditions of possibility for women's oppression, insisting that "the specific working out of this oppression is a subject for historical, not theoretical, investigation."[27]

Vogel thus avoids attributing undue determinative weight to unpaid domestic work. Certainly, she agrees, such work is a common aspect of women's oppression, and the historically dominant means of reproducing labour power at little cost to capital. But neither the gender division of labour nor the family itself constitute the material basis of women's oppression. Rather, the necessary but contradictory relation of the reproduction of labour power to capitalist accumulation does. That is, women's oppression in capitalist society is grounded in a socio-material or structural logic of capitalist reproduction that limits the possibilities for women (and all people) to be free.

Analyzing the household is still important as one site of social reproduction organized according to gendered conventions and relations. There is nothing in this perspective, however, that positions the household as an unvarying institution of patriarchal relations. Households can and do take a variety of forms, including single-parent, same-sex, or group homes of unrelated individuals. They can be centres of oppression and conflict, or characterized by warmth and support; and usually they are both, "bound together in a dynamic combination that is not necessarily fixed."[28] The household is better understood as an historically evolving, socially, culturally, and geographically located institution—albeit one that, crucially, is imbricated in a contradictory dynamic vis-à-vis capital.

Moreover, the household is not the only site of labour power's reproduction. Vogel mentions "labor camps, barracks, orphanages, hospitals, prisons, and other such institutions."[29] And there are many more, not least among them the community-based organizations that Claudia Jones and other black feminists mention as the focus of much African American women's activism. Many of these, such as schools, hospitals, and the homes of middle class white employers of black and immigrant housekeepers and childminders, are sites of paid work. These forms of social reproductive labour—just like unpaid housework—are organized in and through social hierarchies. And not only through gender hierarchies. The full scope of labour power's reproduction is governed through local, national, and global regimes that draw on various forms of oppression in ways that tend to reinforce them. In ensuring the social reproduction of certain communities is more precarious and under-resourced than others, they facilitate the reproduction of an unequal, internally divided workforce.

The point is that all processes of social reproduction (not just those in individual households) come up against capital's hostility to life—if for no greater reason than that the vast majority of the resources essential to reproducing life (the means of subsistence) are owned and controlled by capital and the capitalist state. And all the work that goes into producing this and the next generation of workers (inside and outside of patriarchally organized households) is caught up in specific social relations of oppression that are not directly subject to capitalism's direct control but are nonetheless caught in the crosshairs of this contradictory dynamic.

CAPITALISM'S COMPLEX SOCIAL REPRODUCTIVE LABOUR

Mies and Federici capture the processes by which such dynamics play out in their analyses of global capitalism. They propose that capital colonizes not just the "productive" resources of the "Third World," but crucially, its "reproductive" resources, including peasant and common lands, and women's (largely unpaid) labour and bodies. International "development" projects, such as the World Bank's Structural Adjustment Programs, forced people off the land and reorganized domestic production relations often by undermining subsistence farming, the bulk of which is performed by women.

This "freeing" of the world's population for waged work cannot be accomplished without intensifying racial and patriarchal violence, from dowry murders and trafficking sex workers, to shifting women from the productive center of their societies to the newly privatized, devalued margins.[30] As Federici eloquently puts it:

> Capitalism must justify and mystify the contradictions built into its social relations—the promise of freedom vs. the reality of widespread coercion, and the promise of prosperity vs. the reality of widespread penury—by denigrating the "nature" of those it exploits: women, colonial subjects, the descendants of African slaves, the immigrants displaced by globalization.[31]

Such coercion and denigration are the means by which ruling classes navigate the necessary-but-contradictory relationship of capitalistically "productive" to reproductive labour. And that navigation occurs not only in workplaces, under capital's direct command, where it is tailored to grind maximum surplus value out of paid workers. It occurs as well in the spaces and times of social reproduction, where usually capitalists are not in a position of immediate and direct domination. (I say "usually" because distance from capital's domination is not pre-given fact but is a matter of history. The social reproduction of enslaved peoples, labour camp internees, and migrant workers housed by their employers are examples of capitalists exercising much more direct control over workers' lives than they do over those workers who live in individual private households.)

One way to think about it is to consider that bodies matter to capital. Capitalists buy *labour power*, not labour, not the labourer. But labour power necessarily comes with a body attached to it. While it is possible to *imagine* a capitalism in which a single type of body is set to work—all well fed, white, straight, biologically male perhaps—that's not how capitalists have *in fact* managed. Actually existing capitalism (as opposed to a theoretical model existing only in our imaginations) developed through a reliance upon those social oppressions that divide and subjugate bodies according to "race," gender, sexuality, and more. This is precisely what Sadie Alexander points out when she argues that mass production in the United States was only possible in many industries because African

American women were paid such low wages.[32] Industry's profits, she observes, accrued not just from workers but from particular types of workers—workers whose bodies were black and female. For such bodies to be available to capitalists, the ruling class needs to sustain and reinforce racist and patriarchal practices and relations that degrade some bodies more than others.

Thus, while *all* workers are alienated from their humanity when they sell their labour power to a capitalist, the degradation involved in that alienation differs in degree and intensity. The oppressive practices and institutions that sustain that differential dehumanization ensure that workers are more-or-less precarious, more-or-less able and willing to work at dangerous or dirty or low-paying jobs. Social oppression is not called into being by capital—but neither does it unfold in a way that is untouched by capital. The forces of social oppression both shape and are shaped by the capitalist tendency to reduce life to labour power. That is, racism, sexism, and heterosexism (and the resistance they spawn) organize the institutions and practices of life-making in ways that are constantly articulated to—but not necessarily beholden to—capital's need for workers. But not just for any workers. For a socially differentiated (paid and unpaid) workforce.

This socially differentiated workforce reinforces and sustains the conditions for capitalist accumulation in two ways. First, it keeps the costs of social reproduction lower by ensuring some people take on that labour for free or at a low wage. Second, it ensures a steady supply of sufficiently marginalized and precarious workers prepared or forced to accept waged work that is unregulated, unhealthy, and poorly paid. While the resurgence of social reproduction feminism in the 1970s attended to the gendered dimensions of such processes (specifically processes of unpaid domestic labour), more recently attention has turned to the multiple and complexly intersecting range of social oppressions that shape many different processes reproducing workers.

This work brings into view far more than just private households. It brings into view, among other things, processes of dispossession of Indigenous communities, public policies and social practices that exclude or deny transgendered sexualities, ecological destruction of the means of subsistence and systems of migrant and forced labour. And it prompts us to consider how such processes help discipline bodies to capital's mandate of accumulation, and how resisting them is part of the project of dismantling capitalism.

To focus on the example of migration: transnational migration has a long history as a means of meeting capital's appetite for relatively impoverished and degraded bodies willing to sell their labour power for a low wage.[33] Today, there are more than 200 million migrant workers tending the fields, homes, and factories in countries they've travelled to in order to work. War, colonialism, industrial development, debt, and (human-made) ecological disasters have uprooted Indigenous communities and subsistence farmers, forcing millions to navigate the racist, sexist systems that police national borders and organize migration systems. It is through such processes that migrant workers lose their ostensible "freedom" and that capital succeeds in "denigrating the 'nature' of those it exploits."[34]

Attention to the social reproduction of migrant labour highlights the capitalist tendency to separate the processes of life-making from the processes of capital accumulation. Migrant workers are raised and trained in countries and regions other than the (often more affluent) countries and regions that receive them.[35] This geographic distance traversing social and political hierarchies reduces the costs to capitalists in the receiving country for migrant workers' past social reproduction. Not only do "women across the world produce the workers [that] keep the global economy in motion," the costs involved for any publicly delivered education, healthcare, and training they may have received prior to migrating are paid by other nations' or regions' taxes.[36]

At the same time, however, migrant regimes also tend to collapse the distance between social reproduction and capital accumulation. Because migrant workers often live in housing and rely on means of transportation owned or paid for by their employer, capitalists can exercise greater control over how, when, and with what they reproduce their lives. Denied the same rights as citizen workers, often crowded into substandard housing, provided little or no healthcare, and in many cases, unable to live with their own partners and children, migrant workers are frequently more dependent upon and therefore more beholden to their employer for survival than citizen workers tend to be.

The ruling class and its state are thus constantly negotiating the separation of life-making from capitalist value creation. It is not a pre-given, static, or stable separation that can be easily mapped in spatial terms. Rather, it is dynamic and relational, with two opposing tendencies of separation and convergence. Alessandra Mezzadri emphasizes the latter of these tendencies in her discussion of migration within national borders and the (re)production of what is too often presumed to be India's "'natural' comparative advantage" in the world market, cheap labour. Emphasizing the embodied and geo-social spatialization of productive and reproductive labour, she argues that the "subjugation of the Indian working poor is first and foremost realized across realms of reproduction, hence tightly anchoring labour exploitation to wider forms of social oppression."[37]

Mezzadri cites the extensive informalization of employment (93 percent of the Indian workforce), bonded and contracted labour practices, and rural/urban migration patterns as creating a terrain on which social oppressions of caste, gender, and regional inequality ensure that "the lives of the working poor remain entangled across ... 'old' and 'new' poverty cycles, in the context of their highly mobile, multi-local livelihoods."[38] And as labour becomes ever cheaper to reproduce, it also becomes in fact "disposable"—a point Melissa Wright also makes with respect to Mexico's internal migrants, women working in maquiladoras. That is, there comes a point at which labour is socially reproduced at the barest minimum costs, at which the simultaneous reproduction of human life and the production of capital is less of a contradiction. Federici puts it this way: "the destruction of human life on a large scale has been a structural component of capitalism from its inception, as the necessary counterpart of the accumulation of labor power, which is an inevitably violent process."[39]

CONCLUSION

In summary, precarious workforces do not come into being magically or naturally. They are *produced*. In a global system already differentiated along a hierarchically ordered scale of nation states, regional trading blocs, and manufacturing centers, and in which people are dispossessed of the resources needed to reproduce themselves, capitalists have both the means and the motivation to shape the life-making processes of those whose labour they depend upon. Their immediate agendas may not prevail in every context, but the pressure to organize social reproduction through certain types of households, education, healthcare, urban planning, migration systems, and other social policies is ever present. It is systemic. As is the tendency to rely on coercive institutions and practices that discipline the population and facilitate people's dispossession and resettlement. It is in negotiating and shaping these processes of life-making to meet their needs for certain types of workers that ruling classes reinforce and reshape racist, sexist, and other oppressive forms of domination.

But even as capital dominates life-making in these ways, it does not exert absolute control. Bodies can and do resist degradation. Lives can be organized against capital. Life and life-making are fundamentally about the practical human activity through which people meet their current needs and imagine new possibilities—be they pursuing food and shelter or love, play, and rest. And it is precisely because social reproductive labour is distinct from capitalistically "productive" labour, that it can and does resist the alienating and life-thwarting pressures capital applies. There are, however, two schools of thought within social reproduction feminism about how that resistance is best organized, a distinction that flows from a disagreement about how to theorize social reproductive labour's relation to value creation. I untangle that value debate in the next chapter—and show why its resolution matters to forging a robustly anti-oppression socialist politics.

8

The Social Reproduction Strike: Life-Making Beyond Capitalism

Anna Wheeler and William Thompson laid the foundation of the social reproduction feminism trajectory by insisting that "women's work" be counted as part of the overall production of social wealth. In so doing, they pushed feminist discussions about labour beyond the rational-humanist parameters of earlier feminism, into the realm of political economy. This groundwork makes it possible to shift the analytic focus from the gender division of labour to the relation between "women's work" (social reproductive labour) and waged, capitalistically "productive" (value-producing) work.

Most socialist feminists since then have not fully appreciated the power of Wheeler's and Thompson's insight. While they have pointed out how capitalism presupposes the separation of production from reproduction, they have tended to attribute women's oppression to the gender division of labour that attends that separation. Citing women's dependency on men, their isolation in the private sphere, and the drudgery of the work itself, socialist feminists have generally theorized women's labour in the same rational-humanist terms that characterize equality feminism. Linking this critique to a political-economic critique of capitalism (itself understood essentially as a system of "productive" labour), critical equality feminism has produced tendencies toward dualism and class reductionism within socialist feminism.

Others, however, have periodically and partially challenged that theoretical trajectory. In different ways and to different degrees, they have grappled with the political-economic significance of "women's work" to sustaining capitalism. While such efforts were brusquely dismissed in the 1940s by Communist Party leaders, they could not be repressed in the 1970s when social reproduction feminism became, for the first time, a major pole of attraction and debate within socialist feminist circles. Having moved beyond an overly narrow concern with unpaid housework toward more complex and nuanced understandings of the coercive underbelly of capitalist value creation, social reproduction feminists today share a broad theoretical conviction that social oppressions are systemic, grounded in capitalism's necessary-but-contradictory relation of productive to social reproductive work.

Despite identifying a common nexus of problems that this perspective reveals, however, socialist feminists have still not resolved earlier debates about how best to untangle the relation between social reproductive and capitalistically "productive" labour. This chapter addresses that persistent point of disagreement, and the distinct analytic inflections and political conclusions it generates. I take this up here not simply because it is an abiding theoretical question, but because its resolution matters. It matters if we want to convince others of the need for and possibility of forging a truly inclusive class politics that can transcend capitalist relations once and for all. The chapter thus concludes with a discussion of the corresponding political perspectives, making a case for the theoretical political orientation that emphasizes the possibilities of life-making and resistance to capital within multiple forms of working class struggles—the theory and politics advanced, for instance, by the Feminism for the 99% initiative.

SOCIAL REPRODUCTIVE LABOUR AND THE QUESTION OF VALUE

The social reproduction feminist trajectory branched into two related but distinct theoretical orientations. These can be distinguished by the responses of each to the question: Does the work that goes into producing labour power create the actual value that capitalists then appropriate when they sell the products of waged labour? Mary Inman, various contributors to the Domestic Labour Debate, and those involved in the international Wages for Housework (WfH) campaign all propose that it does. Domestic work, they claim, ultimately produces the exchange value of the product of waged labour (the commodity). It does so, many suggest, because it produces the commodity labour power that, when sold to capitalists, produces value. But the relation of the social reproductive worker to capital is obscured by the wage (which appears to be paid only for work done directly for capital) as well as by the family (which provides emotional and ideological cover for what is an essentially oppressive material condition). Because unpaid household labour is capitalistically "productive," they insist, capitalists don't only *depend* upon those whose labour reproduces this and the next generation of workers; they directly *exploit* them.[1]

This perspective developed within autonomist Marxism, a tradition that emerged among radical intellectuals connected to 1960s struggles of Turin auto workers. Responding to the failures of Communist Party leadership, and influenced by the wave of student and feminist struggles, the autonomists moved from an overriding focus on the workplace to seeing capitalism as a totalizing system that organizes *all* members of society (housewives, students, and the unemployed along with waged workers) in the production of wealth that it then appropriates.[2] Mario Tronti introduced the term "social factory" in his 1962 book, *Factory and Society*, to capture the idea that capital *subsumes* all society to the logic of accumulation.[3] Maria Dalla Costa, Silvia Federici, and others pushed the autonomist analysis in a feminist direction by emphasizing that the capitalist subsumption of unwaged labour (for example, housework) requires, sustains, and shapes women's unfreedom.

The WfH campaign also embraced and further developed the autonomist political strategy, which calls on workers to refuse work. Capital thrives on value creation. Accordingly, if workers stop engaging in "productive" labour (that is, if they stop creating value), they deprive capital of its lifeblood. And because all work is "productive"—because, as Federici states, "every moment of our lives functions for the accumulation of capital"—refusing housework and social reproductive labour more broadly conceived also obstructs the creation of value.[4] The WfH campaign therefore called on women to do just that, to walk away from housework. It linked this strategy to the wage demand as a means of emphasizing housework's value, and the impossibility of its full recompense under a capitalist system. The refusal of housework was also intended as a refusal of its commodification (through the hiring of nannies, for instance) and of its organization by the state (through social services).[5] The WfH campaign goal was to "break the whole structure of domestic work" by highlighting all that the wage obscured: capitalists' exploitation of women's unpaid and unfree labour.[6]

Other socialist feminists who conceive of unpaid social reproductive work as capitalistically "*un*productive" also call on women to "refuse" work. However, this group (which I will call the Marxian social reproduction school, or Marxian school for short) defines that refusal differently.[7] I explore that political difference after more closely comparing the ideas informing it.

The Problem of Value

Unconvinced by autonomism, the Marxian school embraces and develops a classically Marxist conception of capitalism. Capitalistically "productive" labour, according to Marx, is that which directly creates value. Value is determined in the process of producing goods and services for exchange (or commodities). In other words, *it is created when the product of labour is destined for sale on the market.* But this is not the case when people take on (unpaid and much paid) social reproductive labour.[8] Such labour certainly contributes to creating a commodity, labour power. But it does so by producing things to be consumed—things that support life (not capital) in the first instance. Its products are meals, clean clothes, community gardens, safe streets, hurricane relief shelters, and mended bones. They are also more ephemeral "things," such as love, attention, discipline, and knowledge that comprise the emotional and social grounding of life. They are *useful* things—things produced not for sale, but to sustain life.

Autonomist Marxist feminists do not generally dispute this reading. Leopoldina Fortunati (who wrote the widely read and cited *The Arcane of Reproduction*) agrees that reproductive labour, which she stresses includes both housework and sex work, produces use value, not exchange value: capital "uses housework as use-value for value."[9] But the meals, clean clothes, sexual pleasure, and so on that it produces, she claims, *transform* into exchange values because they are first consumed by a worker whose labour power later produces value for the capitalist. Thus, social reproductive work, she proposes, *indirectly* creates value.

Insofar as Fortunati means that social reproductive labour is essential to reproducing the conditions that make it possible to create capitalist value, there is no argument with the Marxian school. However, she does not only say that. Fortunati explains that the consumption of use values is a phase in capital's overall process of value creation *because the ultimate product, labour power, is a commodity*. This, she insists, renders it capitalistically "productive" labour. As "productive" workers, housewives and sex workers create not just use value, but value and surplus value. They may do so indirectly, but that indirectness has no apparent bearing on the social form of their work.

Yet, exactly how concrete social reproductive labour transforms from "unproductive" to "productive" is unclear. Fortunati's discussion of the process of its abstraction begins with an assertion:

> If reproduction work … is productive, *then it goes without saying*
> that it too must take on the dual character [for example, abstract and
> concrete] assumed by all other work that produces value. Reproduc-
> tion is not only concrete work, individually necessary and complex, it
> is also abstract human labor, socially necessary and simple.[10]

She then makes two points: (i) social reproductive work shares in a
general character—individual housewives and sex workers labour in
"undifferentiated" ways; and (ii) the labour of one housewife or sex
worker is equal to that of another.

As for the first explanation, this is a conceptual abstraction to be sure,
like any generalization. If I say all trees have trunks, I abstract from
individual trees. But that abstraction proves nothing about the *value*
of the tree, or trunk. Commodity abstraction is something different.
It is a relation of a particular to the general that requires some process
of measuring commensurability. As Marx puts it in the first chapter
of *Capital*, Volume 1, the very exchange, 20 yards of linen = one coat,
requires that qualitatively distinct items (linen and coats) can be rendered
commensurate. The value abstraction of capitalism uses market relations
to transform concrete goods into interchangeable quantities of value
(measured in prices). And this is the problem with Fortunati's second
point. She asserts the commensurability of social reproductive labour
without ever explaining by what measure equality among the different
labours of housewives or sex workers is established. What is the socially
determined standard of commensurability? How is that standard determined? For capitalist commodities, the equation of one labour process
and its commodities is performed by the market. What mechanism does
the same for cooking, sex acts, or cleaning in the home? None of this is
discussed.

Mezzadri's contribution to *Radical Philosophy* provides a recent
example of these unresolved theoretical problems within autonomist
Marxist feminism. She argues that because the rate of exploitation
expands when the costs of social reproduction are reduced, social reproductive labour must be capitalistically "productive" labour. She does
not, however, explain how or why reducing the costs of labour power
to the capitalist (something that can happen for any number of reasons,
from government subsidies to small businesses, to strike-breaking and
back-to-work legislation) in fact *produces* value. How does it, in other
words, make social reproductive labour commensurable and transform

into labour whose value can be abstracted? More significantly, how does it create new value (rather than just redistribute existing value flows)?

While Fortunati and autonomist Marxist feminists more generally grasp that there is a distinction between life and labour power, the significance of that distinction disappears in their analysis of value production. This reflects the autonomist conception of capitalism as a system of *total* domination. All production is value production since the latter is the modus operandi of capitalism. And so, in this reckoning, once one accepts that social reproductive labour is essential to (and therefore "inside") capitalism, it necessarily becomes capitalistically "productive" labour—and is, they reason, fully dominated by or subsumed to capital's imperatives. Any production or life-making *against* or in resistance to capital, it follows, can only take place *outside* the capitalist system (a point I return to in the next section).

According to the Marxian school, because value is determined in producing goods for exchange, and insofar as the products of social reproductive labour have in fact been consumed in the creation and sustenance of life (not capital), that labour cannot be ascribed a capitalistic value. It is "unproductive" in capitalist terms.[11] Granted one is not obliged to follow Marx, and Fortunati and others critique Marx, pointing out that value exists where he believes it does not.[12] But, in this instance, Fortunati clearly thinks she *is* following Marx in determining what constitutes abstract labour (as do Dalla Costa and James who explain, "What we meant precisely is that housework as work is productive in the Marxian sense, that is, as producing surplus value").[13] If autonomist Marxist feminists are to convince us that Marx is wrong about how capitalist value is determined, they need to develop a more coherent critique, one that accurately represents his theory and shows where precisely he errs. Instead, Fortunati substitutes Marx's value theory for an alternative theory of *value transfer* (through consumption), drawing imprecisely and somewhat randomly on Marx's categories.

In the absence of a more convincing theory of value, autonomist Marxist feminism relies on a sort of all-or-nothing logic: because social reproductive labour contributes to capitalist processes of accumulation insofar as it produces the labour power upon which capitalists depend, it *must be* value-producing. Or, put another way: capitalist value is created by "productive" labour, ergo all labour that contributes to the realization of capitalist value is "productive." Labour that is not "productive" does not have a role in the creation of capitalist value because, by definition, it cannot. This is, quite simply, a tautology—one that is rooted in vaguely defined meanings of "productive" labour and "value."[14]

Subsumption and the Social Forms of Labour

The Marxian school of social reproduction feminism observes that Marx did not extend his political-economic critique of capitalism to unpaid social reproductive labour but accepts his value theory as authoritative. Here, value creation is understood to require both forms of labour, those that are capitalistically "productive" *and those that are not.* The latter comprises socially necessary unpaid social reproductive work *and* different forms of paid labour—public sector social reproductive labour as well as other work that is, according to Marx, essential but not directly "productive" (such as banking or certain transportation jobs).[15] Capital's domination of these "unproductive" work processes cannot be denied. But it never totally dominates any work process (even "productive" work).

Labour resists total subsumption by capital precisely because there can be no labour without life—without a living human being, whose life needs can and will assert themselves against capital time and again. For both historical and systemic reasons, however, "unproductive" social reproductive labour *tends to be* less fully subsumed to capital than "productive" labour. To begin, as Vogel, Federici, and others have stressed, capitalist production presumes, but does not directly oversee a great deal of social reproductive labour. Much life-making takes place in times and spaces beyond the immediate imperatives of capitalist value production, and thus beyond the supervision of bosses and their production quotas and disciplining practices. This best describes the *unpaid* work of reproducing this and the next generation of workers. Yet because such labour is *necessary* to the realization of surplus value and because it is performed overwhelmingly by those who are already dispossessed by capital, it is never *simply* outside capitalist processes and discipline. It is inflected with the rhythms and paces of value production, even as it is not directly value-producing: resources for living are constrained by wages (and credit limits); time for eating, sleeping, helping a child with homework, playing, and more is generally prescribed by the waged workday; the pressure to perform well at work often determines whether someone parties all night or goes to the gym and then home to bed.

Nonetheless, the unpaid work of social reproduction is sufficiently "outside" capital to be highly flexible. While performing such labour, many people can, to a significant degree, ignore or resist market disciplining of their lives.[16] They can decide how much time to spend making dinner, or whether to attend a community meeting for a safe-injection site instead of preparing lunches for the next school day. Or they can stay up late and do it all. Such control over the content, pace, and timing of work is considerably less available for paid social reproductive workers who are subject to the disciplinary logic of capitalist accumulation in other ways. Paid domestic workers are generally hired not only to ensure that a household runs according to the socially determined standards that facilitate the reproduction of labour power for capital, but also to facilitate the reproduction of the ruling class. They have less autonomy than stay-at-home parents because they are accountable to an employer who expects the work done in a certain amount of time. The work of public sector school custodians, teachers, personal support workers, nurses, and so on, on the other hand, typically has rigidly regulated standards and schedules, as well as on-site managers and structures of accountability to the capitalist state that employs them.

Yet capitalist domination of these jobs is often less direct than it is in private sector work and therefore *can be* less intense. Consider, for example, public sector teaching in North America. Established in the nineteenth century, in many cases in response to working class demand and eventually supported by the state, schools for young children emerged on the sidelines of capital's involvement. Although accountable to the parish, municipal, or other authorities paying their wages, teachers were not generally subject to capitalist management standards and techniques of increasing productivity. As the need for a literate workforce increased, the state made school attendance mandatory and worked to meet the labour demands of the economy by reshaping curriculum, grading, teacher training, and disciplinary practices. Such measures tended to diminish teacher autonomy. There was (and still is) a limit, however, to the degree to which teachers could be made to improve their "output" (whatever that may mean in a given context).[17] Because public education exists "outside" the spaces and times of capitalist value production, capital's domination of teaching jobs is always mediated by other social authorities and—as I say more about in a moment—by pressures from below as well.

More generally, public sector workers who teach, feed, care for, or otherwise assist in the reproduction of human life are subject—to greater and lesser degrees—to workplace supervision, pressures to work more efficiently, performance reviews, and other disciplining measures familiar to those who work in factories or fast-food restaurants. They often report to governing boards populated by members of the ruling class or are managed through bureaucratic chains of command inflected with the priorities and resources provided by the capitalist state. And increasingly, digital technologies are introduced into these work processes to both speed up and monitor workers' "productivity."[18] All these elements of paid public sector social reproductive work subsume a worker to the logic of capital accumulation and regularly override the logic of life-making or meeting human need.

The degree of subsumption, however, varies so widely *precisely because such work is capitalistically "unproductive."* Most significantly, because the product is another human life, social reproductive work tends to be socially interactive in nature. Its "product" can and does talk back, behave in ways that may or may not further the goals of the worker (or the worker's boss). A student who hasn't eaten or had enough sleep cannot learn as well as one who has—regardless of the pressures a teacher is under to submit higher test scores. A patient develops an infection during a routine surgery and ends up spending a week rather than a day in the hospital, requiring more care by more attendants and more administrative and custodial resources than it takes to produce the average healthy human being.

Such scenarios drive home the point that the production of life regularly requires resisting the subsumption of life to capital. And when the workers involved are "unproductive" workers (not hired by private, for-profit companies), they are more able, and sometimes have no choice but to, override capitalist imperatives. Depending upon the degree of autonomy they enjoy, they can even make a point of prioritizing life needs over capital. For example, teachers will often play with and care for their students, not to improve test scores but to address a child's need for attention, fun, and love. A personal support worker paid to dress an elderly client might take extra time to fix the client's makeup or help with setting their room straight for the same reasons. Of course, such workers might choose to ignore or be ill-equipped to deal with those needs as well. But the point is that while there are certainly pressures from above to speed up and shortchange the processes of life-making, public sector social reproduction workers experience pressures from below to do the opposite: they confront and negotiate the needs of the people they are helping to reproduce as part and parcel of their daily work. And in the process, they can establish connections with others that cut against the alienating tendencies of capitalism, emotionally and intellectually investing in their work and the "product" of their labour—despite being immersed in capitalist relations and against the disciplining pressures of management and/or technology.[19]

Relatedly, because such workers produce life not value (albeit under a disciplinary regime of wage labour), it is impossible to capitalistically measure their output. Unlike Google or Amazon, which depend upon market sales to determine the productivity of their workforce (and therefore the standards of productivity to impose), school board trustees have no reliably objective measure to determine how much knowledge a child absorbs. They can, and do, aspire to these—by comparing standardized test scores and school dropout rates among other things. And they use these market "proxies" to discipline teachers. Similarly, hospital management might use time studies to regulate orderlies bathing a patient, or cafeteria workers distributing meals. Such practices facilitate the subsumption of the worker to capitalist imperatives—but not with the degree of rigidity and exactness that they do in the "productive" sector because there is no capitalist value attached to the product life.[20]

This admittedly schematic taxonomy of labour forms is not intended to be the last word on subsumption and the social forms of labour. Indeed, research on this question from a social reproduction feminism perspective is sparse. My goal here is simply to illustrate why the Marxian school insists that capitalist subsumption is *not* a totalizing process, and how that perspective can be understood in relation to the differentiation between "unproductive" social reproductive labour and "productive" labour within capitalist relations. There may be a totalizing tendency at work, but concrete labour can never be fully identical with its abstract form, and the discrepancy between the two will generally be greater where the direct imposition of value imperatives is not available.[21] For it is only by highlighting the co-existence of—and contradictions between—"productive" and "unproductive" labour within the process of value creation that we can grasp how *all* workers (be they reproducing labour power or making capitalist commodities) can and do resist capitalism's relentless degradation of life *despite* their everyday existence as capitalist subjects.

And that is why resolving this question of theory matters politically. The theoretical disagreements just outlined lead autonomist Marxist feminism to conceptualize the possibilities for resistance as existing beyond or outside capitalist relations, in the creation of alternative spaces to capitalism; the Marxian school looks instead toward struggles to break the system from within. This requires, among other things, drawing on and continuing to develop the anti-oppression politics of a renewed social reproduction feminism perspective in order to forge and strengthen ties of solidarity across community and workplace movements. Along with tracing the ties between theoretical and political differences, the next section proposes that the autonomist Marxist feminist strategic focus on building alternatives to capitalism forfeits fertile political ground. It fails to highlight the potentialities of mass movement building *across* productive and reproductive sectors for forging new ways of life-making while also confronting capital on its own terrain.

FROM THEORY TO POLITICS:
SOCIAL REPRODUCTION FEMINIST STRATEGIES

Both approaches discussed here hold that because the reproduction of labour power is at one and the same time the reproduction of life, it is always possible and often necessary for the forces of life to assert themselves against the forces of capital. As Federici writes:

> Highlighting the reproduction of "labor power" reveals the dual character and the contradiction inherent in reproductive labor and, therefore, the unstable, potentially disruptive character of this work. To the extent that labor power can only exist in the living individual, its reproduction must be simultaneously a production and valorization of desired human qualities and capacities, and an accommodation to the externally imposed standards of the labor market.[22]

Those "desired human qualities and capacities" constitute an immense well of "practical human activity" from which new societies can be forged—societies that put human need ahead of profit. Autonomist Marxist feminism and the Marxian school further agree that the social reproduction strike plays a key role in resisting capital and forging new societies. Where they differ is in their *conception* of the social reproduction strike—what it precisely takes to mobilize the forces of life to disrupt capital's power to impose the "standards of the labor market."

Federici has been at the forefront of advancing a renewed political vision that draws on the theory and politics of refusal that informed the WfH campaign. In a 2008 article, she calls for a "reopening of a collective struggle over reproduction" through which workers assert control over "the material conditions of our reproduction and creat[e] new forms of cooperation around this work *outside of the logic* of capital and the market."[23] She advocates carving out collective spaces beyond capital's reach wherein people socially reproduce themselves and their communities. For once outside capitalism, she argues, it is possible to forge new, collective, ways of living and producing.

Federici has in mind communal kitchens, farms, and land occupations (citing recent Latin American initiatives as examples), as well as market-alternative trading systems for healthcare, childcare, and other social services. These are "cooperative forms of reproduction [that enable people] to survive despite their very limited access to monetary income."[24] Careful not to endorse just any cooperative venture, she elaborates upon and qualifies the concept of a *revolutionary* commons in a 2014 article written with George Caffentzis. A revolutionary notion of the commons not only refuses the logic of capitalism but also works "to transform our social relations and create an alternative to capitalism." To that end, the authors outline six political and logistical principles informing a "commons against and beyond capitalism," which establish an embryonic post-capitalist set of relations.[25]

Kathi Weeks advances a similar vision of moving beyond capital, although she proposes somewhat different means. Weeks follows Jean Baudrillard's critique of Marx's insistence that humans are fundamentally producers. She suggests that as "the practical and ideological position of abstract labor … [this claim is] a mythology internal to and … ultimately supportive of the work society," or capitalism. Insofar as Marxist and socialist feminist politics begin from this same premise, they exhibit similar "productivist tendencies." In revaluing unwaged work and care, socialist feminists end up "replicat[ing] the very ideas about the moral virtues of work" that capitalism relies upon. Resistance to capital, counsels Weeks, requires instead that movements refuse work—that they collectively reject work's domination of life and instead develop the possibilities of the "creative powers of social labor."[26]

Weeks highlights the campaign for a Universal Basic Income (UBI) as an example of such a politics. A decent, unconditional guaranteed income, she suggests, allows people to opt out of waged work and force employers to increase wages and "pursue opportunities for pleasure and creativity that are *outside* the economic realm of production," including opportunities to "recreate and reinvent relations of sociality, care and intimacy."[27] Such prefigurative relations are not ends in themselves but a means of revealing how capitalist society is dominated by work, and how work is organized through a gender division of labour and the naturalization of the family. That is, the call for UBI is, like the WfH campaign before it, intended as a "perspective and provocation" as much if not more than as a demand in its own right.[28]

The above summary leaves much out of two important analyses. I hope it provides sufficient context, however, to trace the connection between their political proposals and the theory that informs them. Both Weeks and Federici support building alternatives to capitalism as a path to revolution, seeing these as crucial spaces in which people can develop prefigurative relations that put the needs of human life ahead of those of capital. They see in such spaces an immanent counter-power to capital. By consciously developing value-alternative communities and initiatives, people grasp their own agency as makers of the world and develop dis-alienated ways of relating to each other and the things they produce. Such alternatives must be established outside or against capital because capitalism is a totalizing system that flattens any differentiation between capitalistically "productive" and "unproductive" labour. For the production of use values to dominate—for production to serve life not capital—workers must escape capitalist relations and organize their labour according to revolutionary principles of cooperation.

This is the essence of the strike, or the refusal to work, as defined by autonomist Marxist feminists. It is a *withdrawal* from the capitalist system and the development of a new, classless, economic system. It paints a scenario in which capital is resisted in a piecemeal and cumulative fashion, as more and more people develop capital-resistant modes of living or getting things done. The counter-power to capitalism emerges because members of the revolutionary commons gain greater control over the conditions of their social reproduction and embrace alternative ways of being that resist the "work society." It is here, within communities and initiatives "outside" capitalism, where members discover and nurture the "creative powers of social labor."

For the Marxian school, the social reproductive strike is also incredibly important. In a "manifesto" written to explain and advance the political perspective informing many of the recent International Women's Day strikes, Cinzia Arruzza, Tithi Bhattacharya, and Nancy Fraser offer a rationale that echoes the autonomist Marxist feminism position: "By withholding housework, sex, smiles, and other forms of gendered, invisible work, [striking women] are disclosing the indispensable role of social reproductive activities in capitalist society." The strike broadens our understanding of who works to sustain capitalism—and therefore of who comprises the "working class"—while also "disclosing the unity of 'workplace' and 'social life.'" And, as Weeks and Federici also stress, Arruzza, Bhattacharya, and Fraser insist that the social reproductive strike represents a space of creativity, a space where "the impossible" can and must be demanded.[29]

For both political perspectives, then, the social reproductive strike is a powerful weapon in the struggle against capital. The Marxian school departs from autonomist Marxist feminism, however, in its definition of what constitutes a strike, and more significantly, in its conception of how the strike poses a threat to capital. According to the authors of *Feminism for the 99%: A Manifesto*, the strike is not only or even primarily a withdrawal from capitalist relations. Certainly, many anti-capitalist camps, occupations, and communal kitchens Federici refers to are examples of social reproductive strikes which, according to this perspective, should be supported. But for the Marxian school, so too are those anti-capitalist social movements that make demands on the state without also creating worker production or trading cooperatives. As are walkouts and militant protests of paid social reproductive workers in the public sector. The *Manifesto* celebrates, for example, workplace- and community-based protests for better schools, healthcare, housing, transportation, and environmental protections. And it stresses the importance of building solidarity across such struggles.

Many of these strikes do not refuse work in the sense discussed by Federici and Weeks. But they nonetheless make claims for democratic and collective control of the conditions of (re)production. They are examples of people who collectively insist on putting need over profit by demanding that the resources for social reproduction be expanded—who attempt, that is, to take life back from capital. For the Marxian school, then, the strike is a moment of collective *struggle against* capital. It is not so much the forging of an *alternative to or a way beyond* capital, even though it can and often does engender the creativity and social bonds that revolutionary cooperatives can engender (a point I return to below). Rather, these strikes are fundamentally about building a mass movement capable of confronting capital on its own terrain.

That terrain is organized by capital and the capitalist state. Although both forms of labour are necessary to sustaining capitalism, according to this perspective, "productive" labour does not hold the same relation to capital as "unproductive" labour. On the one hand, that means that conventional workplace-based strikes in capitalistically "productive" industries are critical to any anti-capitalist movement. One cannot adequately threaten the ruling class by organizing resistance *solely* around social reproductive labour strikes. On the other hand, because social reproductive labour is not capitalistically "productive" labour and is managed to a large degree by the state, the fight against capital must also engage the state—through attempts to assert the priorities of life over capital whether in paid or unpaid sites of social reproductive labour.[30]

Not only does the Marxian school identify the need to develop anti-capitalist struggles on multiple fronts, it prioritizes building bridges between those fronts. Practically, this means figuring out ways for workplace strikes to incorporate anti-oppression politics, and for anti-oppression strikes to incorporate workplace-based demands. Examples of this cross-fertilization include Black Lives Matter organizing with some Kentucky teachers to oppose that state's racist so-called gang bill (HB 169) as part of their strike actions.[31] Or the New York Teamsters transformation into a "sanctuary union" which protects its members from being detained and deported by immigration authorities.[32] By *engaging* with anti-capitalist struggles both "inside" and "outside" capitalist social relations, strikes not only can expand the "partial protection for some from capital's inherent tendency to cannibalize social reproduction."[33] They can also—and this is a point that the theoretical commitments of autonomist Marxist feminism fails to make evident—create *alternative communities of struggle* wherein bonds of solidarity are forged and strikers develop creative ways of meeting people's needs.

That is, strikes do not have to be exercises in revolutionary commons to model alternative ways of organizing life-making. The potential to unleash creative energies and ideas about how to build a better world and engender social bonds to counter the alienation and isolation of capitalist subjectivity is inherent in the very act of organizing with others to improve control over the conditions of work and life. Perhaps the most vivid recent example of this come from the 2018 wave of education worker strikes to hit the United States. Eric Blanc's interviews with more than a hundred people involved in the West Virginia, Arizona, and Oklahoma strike movements lead him to conclude that strikers were "profoundly transformed" by their participation.[34] They connected in new ways with co-workers they had barely known and had little in common with culturally and ideologically; they strategized, waved placards, shared meals, chanted, sang, and camped out on the state legislative grounds together; they jointly endured moments of disappointment, debate and defeat, and even bigger moments of celebration. And they connected in new ways with the communities they worked in as passersby honked and waved in support, as strangers identifying them by their distinctive red T-shirts approached them in grocery stores to thank them for their job action, and as students and parents stood on their lines and rallied in support. In the words of Arizona teacher Noah Karvelis, interviewed by Blanc:

> Since the strike, there's a definite sense of solidarity that wasn't there before. When you go into school and see all of your coworkers in red, it's like they're saying, "I'm with you, I got you." It's hard to even sum up that feeling. You used to go in to school, do your thing, and go home. Now if there's a struggle, we go do something about it because we're in it together. It's not just that there are a lot more personal friendships—we saw that we had power.[35]

Such solidarity did not magically appear. It had to be built. The strikers were divided by all the usual social cleavages. Not all teachers were in the union and most were white. They differed in political allegiance, religious affiliation, and income (in West Virginia bus drivers, cafeteria cooks, custodians, and other support staff walked out as well). Moreover, as social reproductive workers in the public sector, the walkout risked creating a wedge between themselves and the community they served. Rather than deny these divisions, organizers and strikers consciously addressed them—figuring out imaginative ways of addressing needs and drawing people in: bilingual signs and chants, GoFundMe sites to help lower-income strikers make ends meet, soliciting food donations, and delivering care packages for families who otherwise rely on school lunches. As Kate Doyle Griffiths observes, strikers temporarily and partially reorganized the relations of social reproductive labour "on the basis of workers control for the benefit of the wider working class" while also fostering solidarity with community members.[36] And although strikers did not generally politicize around racial issues, Blanc notes, they were self-consciously inclusive and won the support of the majority black and brown student base and their families through their calls for increased school funding and (in Arizona) opposition to cuts to Medicaid and services for those with disabilities.[37] These are not-so-small and incredibly important examples of how strikers organize new ways of life-making, ways that defy the alienating, individualizing experiences of everyday life under capitalism.

These are the lessons Arruzza, Bhattacharya, and Fraser take from struggle:

> Struggle is an opportunity and a school. It can transform those who participate in it, challenging our prior self-understandings and reshaping our view of the world. It can deepen our comprehension of our own oppression—what causes it, who benefits, and what must be done to overcome it. The experience of struggle can also prompt us to reinterpret our interests, reframe our hopes, and expand our sense of the possible. It can induce us to revise prior understanding of who are our allies and who are our enemies. It can broaden the circle of solidarity among the oppressed and sharpen their antagonism to the oppressors.[38]

There is nothing within autonomist Marxist feminism that suggests this form of organizing should not be supported—and those associated with the tradition have been supportive of the teachers' strike and similar struggles. Rather, my point is that a theory of capital that conflates all labour with "productive" labour has little to say about the strategic role of such strikes. Because autonomist Marxist feminism understands value to be created everywhere, *all* places play the same role in resisting capital. There is, in other words, *from capital's perspective*, little to differentiate a walkout by Walmart workers from a politicized, cooperative community kitchen. Both stop the creation of value; both refuse capitalist ethics and organization of work. As a result, there is no compelling or clear necessity to promote political strategies to bridge struggles on multiple fronts.

Federici and Weeks are indeed relatively silent about whether one should or how one might confront capital on its own terrain. They don't discuss the potential of such strikes to forge social bonds and ways of provisioning and supporting each other that allow us to imagine building a better world is in fact possible. Neither do they have much to say about how their strategies relate to anti-oppression social movements that make demands on the state, and even less to say about building solidarity with trade unionists and others at the point of capitalist production. For example, of the six principles of revolutionary commons Federici and Caffentzis propose, five deal with the internal organization of alternative communities. None mentions the significance of workplace-based struggles to the revolutionary commons project. And only one mentions connecting the project with those who fight for improved state services and resources—a connection the authors endorse as "an ideological imperative" because the state manages collective wealth, which must be reappropriated and public sector workers have a certain, useful, knowledge base.[39]

Weeks, on the other hand, advocates making a demand on the state for UBI while making it clear that the goal is not simply or even necessarily achieving the reform. The demand itself, she explains, is both perspective and provocation. In the same sense that the WfH campaign did not really expect the state to pay housewives wages (because of the threat to capitalism this would pose), Weeks understands that capitalism will not abide UBI. As a result, "it is not the content of the demand but the collective practice of demanding that will determine whether what we win 'will be a victory or a defeat.'"[40] She gestures here to the importance of building mass resistance, but doesn't develop this point. Similarly, although Weeks discusses why a guaranteed basic income could strengthen workers' social power (because it would improve their wage bargaining leverage), she doesn't elaborate on building solidarity among the employed and unemployed. The autonomist Marxist feminism theory points her, and Federici, in a different direction.

CONCLUSION

The Marxian school prioritizes struggle against capital, not because it is particularly combative in outlook. Confrontation, it claims, is an essential political strategy because there can be no form of labour today (cooperative or not) that fully escapes capital's domination—that is not already imbued, more-or-less, with the imperatives of capitalist accumulation.[41] Consider, for instance, that occupations exist on land already defined by capitalist processes of dispossession and accumulation (otherwise what precisely is being *occupied*? or from whom is the land being *claimed* or *protected*?). And commons of any sort are organized within political jurisdictions defined in relation to and largely beholden to capitalists' interests. To be "outside" capital is, by definition, to be determined to some extent by capital. There can only be spaces and times that are, more-or-less, shaped by the logic of capitalist accumulation. Subsumption is, as I argue above, a matter of degree—not a totalizing experience.[42]

It is simply not possible then to refuse work's domination of life—be it through the freedom granted by UBI or through organizing production within revolutionary commons. Rather, work dominates life as a condition of capitalist existence. At the same time, that domination is always susceptible to forms of internal resistance. As we saw in the first chapter of this book, work dominates life because capital has robbed people of the means with which they make life. To move beyond capital then means that workers need to push back against capital's domination of life *within the system itself*—to claim more resources for life-making and fewer for capital. But until we destroy capitalism, we cannot escape it. We are always, everywhere, in struggle with it.

This is why, the authors of the *Manifesto* place so much emphasis on struggle and solidarity. And why they call the strike movement "Feminism for the 99%"—a movement that in drawing into struggle the exploited, dominated, and oppressed forges connections between and among those who have a common interest in creating a new, socialist or post-capitalist, society:

> Feminists for the 99% do not operate in isolation from other movements of resistance and rebellion. We do not separate ourselves from battles against climate change or exploitation in the workplace. Nor do we stand aloof from struggles against institutional racism and dispossession. Those struggles are our own struggles, part and parcel of the struggle to dismantle capitalism, without which there can be no end to gender and sexual oppression.[43]

Building solidarity, in this reckoning, is the strike's means *and* end. Second Wave feminist theory was mistaken, write Arruzza, Bhattacharya, and Fraser, "in treating universal sisterhood as the starting point." Solidarity is, in fact, the goal.[44] Avoiding that mistake requires patiently negotiating ways of working together while respecting the integrity of each sector's organizational and political autonomy. In this, socialist feminists embrace the Combahee River Collective vision of resistance in which one group's "liberation is a necessity not ... an adjunct to somebody else's" while also incorporating those particular struggles into a shared movement aimed at destroying capitalism. Only then can the strike be a widely diverse confrontation with capital on multiple fronts— in the realm of social reproduction *and* "production" without collapsing one struggle into the other. That is, only then does revolutionary strategy entail incorporating multiple forms of resistance to capital through building a mass movement linking struggles in communities and on the streets with those taking place within paid workplaces. Such a movement is diverse but united in its intent to create a world that prioritizes need over profit, that dislodges labour for capital with labour for life.

Afterword

One risk of the way in which I've structured this book is that the reader might close the back cover believing that feminist theories of labour have progressed, along a more or less straightforward line, from wrong-headed equality feminism to somewhat more acceptable critical equality feminism to the ultimate wisdom of social reproduction feminism.

Let me take a moment here to avert that possibility. The three trajectories I outlined are still very much in play today. Equality feminism continues to navigate the mainstream terrain of work and politics in the Global North, often with some success. Having increasingly transformed into the business-friendly feminism discussed in Chapter 6, it nonetheless still conceives of work as a path to women's freedom. The key difference is that now freedom is often defined not just by achieving economic independence from men, but also by achieving a higher class position and salary. While most women would benefit from higher pay and status at work, those who realize this feminist dream to its fullest (the Hillary Clintons or Sheryl Sandbergs of this world, for example) cannot help but do so by squashing the freedom dreams of millions of working class women who do not. But even for the middle class women that Friedan addressed, the equality feminist strategy of creating a "new life plan" that accommodates love, children, and home, on the one hand, and jobs that can help shape the future, on the other, is also achieved on the backs of millions of other, poorer and overwhelmingly racialized, women who cannot imagine such life plans for themselves.

Within the socialist tradition, perspectives continue to shift between critical equality and social reproduction feminisms, resulting in ongoing theoretical confusions outlined in previous chapters. I see the current revival of interest in social reproduction feminism, however, as an opportunity to unpack those confusions, and work toward a more robust theoretical grounding for a transformative politics that places the fight against oppression at the center of the fight against capital. I hope this book provides a theoretical scaffolding that can contribute to such a project—a project that is, I might add, never finished. For theory is not about finding the "right" answers so much as it is about constantly testing ideas against realities to expand understanding of how the world works. As those realities change, so too must theory. That's why the current iterations of social reproduction feminism discussed here are hardly definitive. But they do, I submit, capture something important about today's realities.

Most significantly, they identify and explain the logic behind the necessary but contradictory relation of social reproductive to capitalistically "productive" labour. In so doing, social reproduction feminism today challenges past socialist feminist notions of what work is. To begin, it moves beyond earlier understandings of "women's work," emphasizing that it may be paid or unpaid, performed in households, communities, or paid workplaces. And although it is conventionally gendered, such work does not have to be performed by women. Moreover, it is deeply and intractably implicated in various structures and forces of social oppression that the capitalist state and ruling class more generally help to perpetuate.

Work, itself, in this view is neither good nor bad. It is at the most general level the conscious, affective, sense-laden, creative interaction with the world that Marx observes is the necessary condition and result of human society. Because this "practical human activity" is in and of history, however, it is organized through the social relations that people inherit and constantly create anew. Capitalist social relations organize work in such a way that work tends to dominate life—separating out capitalistically "productive" labour from social reproductive labour, and abstracting from "productive" workers' concrete exertions to create capitalist value and profit.

In attending to the duality of work—its concrete and abstract forms—social reproduction feminism emphasizes the contradictions between value creation and life creation; it draws attention to the fact that while work is always subject to capitalist disciplines, it also always exceeds them. As a result, those engaged in social reproductive labour can and do defy the alienating and life-crushing tendencies of capitalism to assert and create new forms of relations with each other and with the natural world. This is what teachers, hospital workers, community activists, among others, do every day. And when they do it collectively, with a consciousness of building solidarities among oppressed groups whose aim is to take life back from capital, they have a powerful potential to thwart the system that constantly diminishes and degrades the very lives it depends upon. They have the potential, that is, to organize work for life, not capital.

Notes

All websites accessed 29 July 2019.

INTRODUCTION

1. Clare Foran, "Hillary Clinton's Feminist Triumph," *The Atlantic* (July 28, 2016), www.theatlantic.com/politics/archive/2016/07/hillary-clinton-presidential-nomination-dnc/493556/.
2. "Our Platform," International Women's Strike USA (no date), www.womenstrikeus.org/our-platform/.
3. See Cinzia Arruzza, Tithi Bhattacharya and Nancy Fraser, *Feminism for the 99%: A Manifesto* (London: Verso, 2019).
4. Diana Broggi, "Argentina's Popular Feminism," trans. Nicolas Allen, *Jacobin* (March 8, 2019), www.jacobinmag.com/2019/03/argentina-feminist-movement-womens-strike.
5. Class reductionism means prioritizing economic or workplace-based struggles over community-based movements against social oppressions, and dualism refers to the idea that patriarchy and capitalism are parallel systems of exploitation and oppression.

CHAPTER 1: THE LABOUR LENS

1. *Unpaid Care and Domestic Work: Issues and Suggestions for Viet Nam* (Hanoi: United Nations Entity for Gender Equality and the Empowerment of Women, 2016), www.un.org.vn/en/publications/doc_details/534-unpaid-care-and-domestic-work-issues-and-suggestions-for-viet-nam.html, 8; *World Development Report 2012: Gender Equality and Development* (Washington: The International Bank for Reconstruction and Development/The World Bank, 2011), https://openknowledge.worldbank.org/handle/10986/4391, 80.
2. *Women at Work: Trends 2016* (International Labor Organization, 2016), 11, 30–5, www.ilo.org/wcmsp5/groups/public/---dgreports/---dcomm/---publ/documents/publication/wcms_457317.pdf.
3. By women's work I mean quite literally the work women do in the paid and unpaid workforce. Much of this is work conventionally understood as best suited for women (for example, domestic work), but I use the term more broadly. When I refer to more conventional understandings, I add scare quotes ("women's work") or specify women's (paid or unpaid) reproductive, household, or domestic work.
4. Peasant societies, and noncapitalist societies generally, are characterized by people moving relatively seamlessly between instrumental activity (work) and pleasure-seeking activity (play). See Mikhail Bakhtin, *Rabelais and His*

World (Cambridge, MA: MIT Press, 1968); Barbara Ehrenreich, *Dancing in the Streets: A History of Collective Joy* (New York: Henry Holt, 2007); and Cindi Katz, *Growing Up Global: Economic Restructuring and Children's Everyday Lives* (Minneapolis: University of Minnesota Press, 2004).

5. Karl Marx, *Grundrisse: Foundations of the Critique of Political Economy (Rough Draft)*, trans. Martin Nicolaus (Harmondsworth: Penguin Books, 1993), 471; see also Alfred Schmidt, *The Concept of Nature in Marx*, trans. Ben Fowkes (London: New Left Books, 1971), 172. Maria Mies challenges the claim that this direct relationship is "natural," observing that "female productivity is the precondition of male productivity and of all further world-historic development." Along with biologically reproducing societies, she points out, women's work supplies the bulk of subsistence needs. See her *Patriarchy and Accumulation on a World Scale: Women in the International Division of Labour* (London: Zed Books, 2014), 58.

6. To be sure, not all hardships were imposed by feudal masters, as the peasant economy was also vulnerable to famine and plagues. See Rodney Hilton, "Introduction," in *The Transition from Feudalism to Capitalism*, ed. Hilton (London: Verso, 1978).

7. Marx, *Grundrisse*, 471.

8. Rodney Hilton, *Class Conflict and the Crisis of Feudalism*, revised 2nd edition (London: Verso, 1990), 57–8; Silvia Federici, *Caliban and the Witch: Women, the Body and Primitive Accumulation* (New York: Autonomedia, 2004), 26.

9. See T.H. Aston and C.H.E. Philpin, eds., *The Brenner Debate: Agrarian Class Structure and Economic Development in Pre-Industrial Europe* (Cambridge: Cambridge University Press, 1985); and Hilton, *Transition*.

10. Karl Marx, *Capital*, vol. I, 1867 (New York: Vintage Books, 1977), 927–8.

11. See E.P. Thompson, "Time Work-Discipline and Industrial Capitalism," *Past & Present* 38 (December 1967): 56–97; and Jonathan Martineau, *Time, Capitalism and Alienation: A Socio-Historical Inquiry into the Making of Modern Time* (Chicago: Haymarket Books, 2015).

12. Claude Meillassoux, "From Reproduction to Production: A Marxist Approach to Economic Anthropology," *Economy and Society* 1, no. 1 (1972): 93–105.

13. Federici, *Caliban*, 91; see also Thompson, "Time Work-Discipline."

14. Federici, *Caliban*, 100; see also Margaret George, "From 'Good Wife' to 'Mistress': The Transformation of the Female in Bourgeois Culture," *Science & Society* 37, no. 2 (Summer 1973): 152–77; and Moira Ferguson, "Introduction," in *First Feminists: British Women Writers 1578–1799*, ed. Ferguson (Bloomington, IN: Indiana University Press, 1985), 3–6. Federici's important insights hold notwithstanding her tendency to overgeneralize about the witch hunt's connection to burgeoning capitalist relations across Europe from the fifteenth century on. See David McNally, *Monsters of the Market: Zombies, Vampires and Global Capitalism* (Chicago: Haymarket Press, 2012), 45, n. 74.

15. See Wally Seccombe, *Weathering the Storm: Working Class Families from the Industrial Revolution to the Fertility Decline* (London: Verso, 1993).

16. I use the terms labour and work interchangeably throughout the book because the literature I engage with tends to do the same. At the same time, however, I argue that work/labour is internally differentiated between the timeless "practical human activity" that is a condition of all life, and the historically specific capturing of that activity by capital, and its distillation through relations of exploitation and oppression.

17. Karl Marx, *The Economic & Philosophic Manuscripts of 1844*, 1932 (Moscow: International Publishers, 1984), 112, emphases in the original. Marx regularly used the gender-neutral *Mensch*, which his translators recorded as "men" or "man." See Roberta Garner and Black Hawk Hancock, eds., *Social Theory: Continuity and Confrontation. A Reader*, 3rd edition (Toronto: University of Toronto Press, 2014), 39; and Adam Tooze, "Gendered Language in Marx Translation," *Notes on Social Theory* 9 (November 2017), www.adamtooze.com/2017/11/09/notes-social-theory-gendered-language-marx-translation/.

18. Marx, *Capital*, 283.

19. Marx, *Manuscripts*, 111.

20. While claiming nature is inherently social and society is natural, Marx still relies upon common sense meanings of those terms, positing a distinction between geological and physiological things and events (nature) and things and events that have been consciously constructed by and for humans (social). I follow Marx in this usage.

21. For a discussion of animals using tools, see Robert W. Shumaker and Kristina R. Walkup, *Animal Tool Behavior: The Use and Manufacture of Tools by Animals* (Baltimore: Johns Hopkins University Press, 2011).

22. Schmidt, *Concept of Nature*, 169. Jean Baudrillard disputes the claim that work is existential. See his *The Mirror of Production*, trans. Mark Poster (St. Louis: Telos, 1973). Kathi Weeks draws on Baudrillard to critique the "productivist" tendencies of much feminism (see Chapter 2).

23. Marx, *Capital*, 283.

24. See John Bellamy Foster, *Marxist Ecology: Materialism and Nature* (New York: Monthly Review Press, 2000); and Chris Williams, *Ecology and Socialism: Solutions to Capitalist Ecological Crisis* (Chicago: Haymarket, 2010).

25. Karl Marx, *The Eighteenth Brumaire of Louis Bonapart* (1852), Marxist Internet Archive (undated), https://www.marxists.org/archive/marx/works/download/pdf/18th-Brumaire.pdf: 5.

26. Mies, *Patriarchy*, 49, emphasis in the original.

27. Marx, *Manuscripts*, 113.

28. See Mies, *Patriarchy*, 83–90; and Annie McClintock, *Imperial Leather: Race, Gender and Sexuality In the Colonial Context* (New York: Routledge, 1995), 152–5.

29. Mies attributes this increase to colonial profits from exceptionally low wages of Indigenous labour. This is questionable, however, since high profits tend to accrue from technically advanced sectors which colonial plantations were not.

CHAPTER 2: THE RATIONAL-HUMANIST ROOTS
OF EQUALITY FEMINISM

1. Although not widely used until the early 1900s, the term feminism is used today to refer to women's "advocates" in prior centuries. Joan Kelly, "Early Feminist Theory and the 'Querelle des Femmes', 1400–1789," *Signs* 8, no. 1 (Autumn 1982): 4–28, 5, n. 3.
2. Ibid., 11.
3. Ibid., 5; see also Rosalind Brown-Grant, "Introduction," in *The Book of the City of Ladies*, 1405, Christine de Pizan, trans. and ed. Brown-Grant (Harmondsworth: Penguin Books, 1999), xix–xxiii.
4. Utopian socialist feminism emerges in the 1820s and ties women's liberation to the communal reorganization of work, family, and society.
5. Christine de Pizan, *City of Ladies*, 6.
6. Ibid., 57.
7. Ibid., 58.
8. Kelly, "Early Feminist Theory," 14.
9. Ibid., 7. See also Ferguson, "Introduction"; Gerald M. MacLean, "Introduction," in *The Woman as Good as the Man. Or, the Equality of Both Sexes*, François de La Barre, 1677, trans. A.L. and ed. MacLean (Detroit: Wayne State University Press, 1988); George, "From 'Good Wife.'"
10. Ibid., 23.
11. Keith Thomas, "The Double Standard," *Journal of the History of Ideas* 20, no. 2 (April 1959): 195–216; Rodney Hilton, *The English Peasantry in the Later Middle Ages: The Ford Lecture for 1973 and Related Studies* (Oxford: Oxford University Press, 1975), 95–110; Mary Prior, "Women and the Urban Economy: Oxford 1500–1800," in *Women in English Society 1500–1800*, ed. Prior (New York: Routledge, 1985).
12. Prior, "Women," 55, 60–5. John Bellamy Foster and Brett Clark, "Women, Nature, and Capital in the Industrial Revolution," *Monthly Review* (January 2018): 1–24; Ferguson, "Introduction," 3–6. Wage disparity was also likely new: although historical evidence is sparse, Hilton (*English Peasantry*, 102) suggests rural female manual workers earned roughly the same as men at the end of the fourteenth century.
13. Christopher Hill, *The World Turned Upside Down: Radical Ideas During the English Revolution* (Harmondsworth: Penguin Books, 1976), 312. According to Hill, Winstanley recognized that such sexual freedom was not truly available to women who risked becoming pregnant and abandoned by the man responsible.
14. Ibid., 320.
15. George, "From 'Good Wife,'" 172.
16. Cited in Keith Thomas, "Women and the Civil War Sects," *Past & Present* 13 (April 1958): 42–62, 51.
17. Ibid., 49.

18. Mary Astell, "Some Reflections upon Marriage," 1700, in *First Feminists*, ed. Ferguson, 193.
19. Bathsua Pell Makin, "An Essay to Revive the Antient Education of Gentlewomen, in Religion, Manners, Arts and Tongues," 1673, in *First Feminists*, ed. Ferguson, 137.
20. Ferguson, "Introduction," 20. No one seems to know who Sophia was, but the tracts are a "silent rewriting" of the 1677 translation of *De l'égalité des deux sexes* (1773) by François Poullain de La Barre (MacLean, "Introduction," 28).
21. Sarah Scott, *A Description of Millenium Hall*, 1762, ed. Gary Kelly (Peterborough, ON: Broadview Press, 1995), 115.
22. Ferguson, "Introduction," 21.
23. Mary Collier, "The Woman's Labour," 1739, in *First Feminists*, ed. Ferguson, 260.
24. Ferguson, "Introduction," 14.
25. See Janet Todd, "Behn, Aphra [Aphara]," *Oxford Dictionary of National Biography* (September 23, 2014), https://doi.org/10.1093/ref:odnb/1961.
26. Ann Cromartie Yearsley, "A Poem on the Inhumanity of the Slave-Trade," 1788, in *First Feminists*, ed. Ferguson, 395.
27. This radical Lockean theory of property was advanced most prominently by John Thelwall; see Iain Hampsher-Monk, "John Thelwall and the Eighteenth-Century Radical Response to Political Economy," *The Historical Journal* 34, no. 1 (March 1991): 1–20.
28. Gay L. Gullickson, *Unruly Women of Paris: Images of the Commune* (Ithaca, NY: Cornell University Press, 1996), 97–8.
29. Olympe de Gouges, *Les droits de la femme: A la reine* (1791), *Olympe de Gouges* (July 2018), https://www.olympedegouges.eu/rights_of_women.php: Article VI.
30. Cited in Barbara Taylor, *Mary Wollstonecraft and the Feminist Imagination* (Cambridge: Cambridge University Press, 2003), 176, emphasis in the original.
31. Wollstonecraft also stands out from *querelle* feminists for the degree to which she emphasizes women's internalization of feminine irrationality, sparking discussion about whether to read her as a misogynist. See Susan Gubar, "Feminist Misogyny: Mary Wollstonecraft and the Paradox of 'It Takes One to Know One,'" *Feminist Studies* 20 (Fall 1994): 453–73.
32. Mary Wollstonecraft, *A Vindication of the Rights of Men* and *A Vindication of the Rights of Woman*, 1790 and 1792, ed. Sylvana Tomaselli (Cambridge: Cambridge University Press, 1995), 117.
33. Ibid., 90.
34. Taylor, *Mary Wollstonecraft*, 13.
35. Wollstonecraft, *A Vindication*, 265.
36. Ibid., 140–1.
37. Taylor, *Mary Wollstonecraft*, 3, 2, emphasis in the original.
38. Ibid., 168–71.

39. Wollstonecraft would have discussed the question of communal property with other radical democrats. Her second husband, William Godwin, for one, attributed society's ills to the existence of private property. She may even have known about Indigenous communitarianism which Bryson tells us "briefly circulated on both sides of the Atlantic" when Indigenous women came to Britain to protest their "exclusion ... from negotiations with Anglo-American settlers"; Valerie Bryson, *Feminist Political Theory*, 3rd edition (New York: Palgrave Macmillan, 2016), 15.

40. Taylor, *Mary Wollstonecraft*, 166, 167, 172; see also 162–3 and 172–5. Taylor's discussion of Wollstonecraft's political economy is both immensely informative and, at parts, confusing in its vagueness. Acknowledging Wollstonecraft's conservative critique of property, Taylor hints (166, n. 70) that there is more to it than meets the eye, perhaps referring to Wollstonecraft's later writings that are critical of commercial society. Wollstonecraft is not a "proto-socialist," she states, but is nonetheless "link[ed]" to the utopian socialists in their shared egalitarian utopianism (173). See also Barbara Taylor, *Eve and the New Jerusalem: Socialism and Feminism in the Nineteenth Century* (London: Virago, 1983).

41. Wollstonecraft, *Vindication*, 129–30.

42. Ibid., 231.

43. Ibid.

44. Taylor, *Mary Wollstonecraft*, 167, emphasis added. Wollstonecraft vacillates between positive and negative assessments of the poor and working class.

45. Wollstonecraft, *Vindication*, 264.

46. Ibid., 232, emphasis added.

47. Anne K. Mellor, "Righting the Wrongs of Women: Mary Wollstonecraft's *Maria*," *Nineteenth-Century Contexts* 19 (1996): 413–24, 415–16, emphasis in the original. Wollstonecraft doesn't dwell on labour market restrictions for middle and upper class women aside from pointing out that the professions are closed to the "well-educated woman, with more than ordinary talents"; Mary Wollstonecraft, *Mary and Maria*, ed. Janet Todd (Harmondsworth: Penguin Books, 1991), 110.

48. Wollstonecraft, *Mary and Maria*, 63.

49. Mary Hays, "Letter to the Editor of the *Monthly Magazine*," 1797, in *First Feminists*, ed. Ferguson, 418–19.

50. Ibid., 418.

51. Mary Anne Radcliffe, *The Female Advocate: Or an Attempt to Recover the Rights of Women from Male Usurpation* (London: Verner and Hood, 1799), http://ota.ox.ac.uk/text/5092.html, 86.

52. Ibid., 46, 85–6. Radcliffe's history requires some revision. Although comprehensive statistics prior to the 1850s are not available, local records suggest men had indeed taken over brewing, midwifery, millinery, and medicine, but women could be found in tailoring, nursing, and teaching, for example. Women also worked in significant numbers on farms and in cottage industries, as domestic servants, and in factories and mines; see William Stafford, *English Feminists and their Opponents in the 1790s: Unsex'd and*

Proper Females (Manchester: Manchester University Press, 2002), 53, 145; and Joyce Burnett, "Women Workers in the British Industrial Revolution," in EH.Net Encyclopedia, ed. Robert Whaples (March 26, 2008), http://eh.net/encyclopedia/women-workers-in-the-british-industrial-revolution/. Also, the fallen genteel woman was, at the end of the eighteenth century, an anomaly—a popular trope based more in fiction than in reality (Stafford, *English Feminists*, 83).

53. Priscilla Wakefield, *Reflections on the Present Condition of the Female Sex; with Suggestions for its Improvement* (London: J. Johnson, 1798), 125.

54. Ibid., 150, 151. "Vails" and "perquisites" are old English words for gratuities.

CHAPTER 3: SOCIALIST FEMINISM: TWO APPROACHES TO UNDERSTANDING WOMEN'S WORK

1. The about-face is significant but not as radical as it might appear. Engels follows the 1845 passage by denouncing men's unjust rule over women. See Friedrich Engels, *The Condition of the Working Class in England*, 1845 (London: Panther Books, 1969), 173–4; and *The Origin of the Family, Private Property and the State*, 1884 (New York: International Publishers, 1972), 50.

2. The term *capitalistically* "productive" signals the Marxian term for labour that produces capitalist value, distinguishing it from more conventional usages referring to labour that produces anything useful.

3. While often considered a utopian socialist, Tristan did not explicitly identify as such. Critical of their political program, she promoted instead working class self-emancipation; see Claire Goldberg Moses, *French Feminism in the Nineteenth Century* (New York: State University of New York, 1984), 110.

4. See Witold Rybczynski, *Home: A Short History of an Idea* (Harmondsworth: Penguin, 1987); and Stephnie Coontz, *The Social Origins of Private Life: A History of American Families 1600–1900* (London: Verso, 1988), 190–8. For a discussion of the uneven and variable patterns through which production for the market moves out of the household in Britain, France, and the United States, see Jane Rendall, *The Origins of Modern Feminism: Women in Britain, France and the United States, 1780–1860* (London: Schocken Books, 1984), 154–61.

5. Moses, *French Feminism*, 177.

6. Bellamy Foster and Clark, "Women," 3.

7. Taylor, *Eve*, 90–1; Rendall, *Origins*, 174–80.

8. These views are associated most closely with the followers of Henri St. Simon and Robert Owen. Charles Fourier did not support communal property.

9. Bryson, *Feminist Political Theory*, 23–4

10. Moses, *French Feminism*, 45–9, 83–7.

11. Taylor, *Eve*, 40. See also Robert Owen, *Lectures on the Marriages of the Priesthood of the Old Immoral World, delivered in the Year 1835, before the Passing of the New Marriage Act*, 4th edition (Leeds: J. Hobson, 1840).

12. Taylor, *Eve*, xii–xviii; Taylor, *Mary*, 173.

13. William Thompson, *Appeal of One Half of the Human Race, Women, Against the Pretensions of the Other Half, Men, to Retain them in Political and thence in Civil and Domestic Slavery*, 1825 (London: Virago, 1983), xxiii. For a discussion of the *Appeal*'s authorship, see Dolores Dooley, *Equality in Community: Sexual Equality in the Writings of William Thompson and Anna Doyle Wheeler* (Cork: Cork University Press, 1996), 179; and Abbie L. Cory, "Wheeler and Thompson's Appeal: The Rhetorical Re-visioning of Gender," *New Hibernia Review* 8, no. 2 (Spring/Summer 2004): 106–20. So devoted to Wheeler was Thompson that he bequeathed her £100 a year and (according to unconfirmable reports) his *bones*—which he instructed to be strung up with the ribs "tipped with silver so that it might present a fashionable appearance" (Richard Pankhurst, "Introduction," in *Appeal*, Thompson, 130). With his estate tied up in court for years, Wheeler appears never to have received the money or the skeletal gift (see Dooley, *Equality*, 51–3 for an authoritative account).

14. Pankhurst, "Introduction," 52–3; Dooley, *Equality*, 56–103.

15. Dooley, *Equality*, 179, 206. See also Terence Ball, "Utilitarianism, Feminism, and the Franchise: James Mill and His Critics," *History of Political Thought* 1, no. 1 (1980): 91–115, 111.

16. Thompson, *Appeal*, 197.

17. Wheeler later suggests that women are not, in fact, weaker than men; cited in Margaret Mcfadden, "Anna Doyle Wheeler (1785–1848): Philosopher, Socialist, Feminist," *Hypatia* 4, no. 1 (1989): 91–101, 96.

18. Thompson, *Appeal*, 298.

19. Ibid., 198, 206.

20. Dooley, *Equality*, 304.

21. This innovation in *theory* did not readily translate into practice. In cooperative societies like New Harmony, Indiana, or New Lanark, Scotland, members collectivized erstwhile "productive" work while clinging to their familiar single-family households, with women doing the bulk of the house and caring work (see Rendall, *Origins*, 218–23).

22. Thompson, *Appeal*, 202.

23. Ibid., 179, 200–1. This passage seems to have escaped Dooley's otherwise careful analysis of the *Appeal*, as she insists that Thompson and Wheeler challenge only "the traditional distribution of work roles ... for women" (*Equality*, 350–1). Similarly, she downplays the significance of their contention that all occupations should be open to both sexes (158–9).

24. Taylor, *Eve*, 37.

25. Thompson, *Appeal*, 203.

26. Dooley points to Wheeler's and Thompson's often dismissive, denigrating attitude toward domestic work, suggesting they did not consider it equally productive with "men's work" (*Equality*, 350). Yet, as she also notes, they are ambivalent in their critique (224–5, 351). My reading is that they question the usefulness of women's domestic labour *within the competitive system*, while also asserting its value and contribution to social wealth in principle.

27. Thompson presumes women would continue to take most responsibility for reproductive labour because their experience in this realm makes them most efficient. See his *An Inquiry into the Principles of the Distribution of Wealth Most Conducive to Human Happiness; Applied to the Newly Proposed System of Voluntary Equality of Wealth* (London: Longman, Hurst, Rees, Orme, Brown, and Green: Pater-Noster-Row, 1824), 46. However, he also suggests that reason, not nature, would decide what division of labour is most beneficial from a utilitarian perspective.

28. Thompson, *Inquiry*, 401. While Thompson's arrogance or naivety are on full display here, he inadvertently makes an important point about the elasticity of social reproductive labour.

29. Ibid., 403, emphasis in the original.

30. Ibid., 401.

31. Owen, *Lectures*, 27, 51.

32. Taylor, *Eve*, 267.

33. See ibid., 265–75. Dorothy Thompson notes that women retreated from politics more generally in the 1840s and after due, among other things, to the supplanting of participatory politics within workers' organizations by "the politics of committee and representative delegations," and to the more frequent use of police to control mass demonstrations; see her *The Chartists: Popular Politics in the Industrial Revolution* (Aldershot: Wildwood House, 1984), 122.

34. Rendall, *Origins*, 171. While the effect of protective legislation on women's labour market participation is debated, there is little doubt it helped consolidate the ideology of gendered labour; see Frieda Fuchs, "The Effects of Protective Labor Legislation on Women's Wages and Welfare: Lessons from Britain and France," *Politics & Society* 33, no. 4 (2005): 595–636.

35. Thompson, *Chartists*, 132.

36. See ibid., 149–50.

37. Cited in Moses, *French Feminism*, 153, 160.

38. Sandra Dijkstra, *Flora Tristan: Feminism in the Age of George Sand* (London: Pluto Press, 1992), 8–10; Moses, *French Feminism*, 19–35.

39. See Dijkstra, *Flora Tristan* for a discussion of Tristan's ambivalence about and martyrdom to the working class.

40. Cited in Joyce Anne Schneider, *Flora Tristan: Feminist, Socialist, and Free Spirit* (New York: William Morrow & Co., 1980), 208.

41. G.D.H. Cole, *Socialist Thought: The Forerunners 1789–1850. A History of Socialist Thought*, vol. 1 (London: McMillan & Co., 1953), 187–8.

42. Arnold Ruge may have taken Marx to her Paris salon (see Dijkstra, *Flora Tristan*, 135–7). Dijkstra makes a case for Tristan's impact on Engels (142–7).

43. Schneider, *Flora Tristan*, 248–9; Moses, *French Feminism*, 107.

44. Flora Tristan, *Promenades dans Londres* (London: W. Jeffs Libraire, 1840), 80–1. Elsewhere, Tristan implies peaceful means may not be sufficient (see Dijkstra, *Flora Tristan*, 171).

45. Flora Tristan, *The Workers' Union*, 1844, trans. and introduction by Beverly Livingston (Chicago: University of Illinois Press, 2007), 79.

46. Ibid.
47. Ibid., 80, 82–3.
48. Ibid., 84–5.
49. The one exception to this attentiveness to class divisions is found her earliest book, *Pérégrinations d'une paria* (Dijkstra, *Flora Tristan*, 50).
50. Flora Tristan, *Flora Tristan: Utopian Feminism. Her Travel Diaries & Personal Crusade*, trans. Doris Beik and Paul Beik (Bloomington, IN: Indiana University Press, 1993), 166, 167.
51. Tristan, *Workers' Union*, 93.
52. Ibid., 123.
53. Kathi Weeks, *The Problem with Work: Feminism, Marxism, Antiwork Politics, and Postwork Imaginaries* (London: Duke University Press, 2011), 8.
54. Ibid., 12.
55. By individualism, I mean the tendency to see individual economic advancement (with attendant changes in personal behaviour, morals, and psychology) as the key to creating a just society.
56. Tristan, *Promenades*, 57 (my translation). Regardless of whether we agree leisure should be used for cultivating minds (as opposed to pursuing more bodily pleasures), Tristan is not positioning *work*, in itself, as a virtue.

CHAPTER 4: EQUAL WORK FOR AND AGAINST CAPITAL

1. Louise A. Tilly and Joan W. Scott, *Women, Work, and Family* (New York: Routledge, 1989); Ruth Milkman, ed., *Women, Work & Protest: A Century of U.S. Women's Labor History* (New York: Routledge, 1985).
2. Since wages for domestic service were comparable to or higher than those for other unskilled or semi-skilled jobs, reasons for this reluctance can only be surmised. Historians often emphasize that paid domestic work was scorned for its "nonproductive," privatized and personalized nature. Certainly, its low social status, unregulated hours, and private, intimate setting increased the potential for abuse. But industrial work shared some of these features. And factory workers had less control over the space and pace of work, qualities domestic servants cited as advantages of their positions. Phyllis Palmer offers an alternative, psychoanalytic, explanation: "sex, dirt, housework, and badness in women are linked in Western unconsciousnesses [such] that white middle-class women sought to transcend these associations by demonstrating their sexual purity and pristine domesticity." See *Domesticity and Dirt: Housewives and Domestic Servants in the United States, 1920–1945* (Philadelphia: Temple University Press, 1989), 138. See also David M. Katzman, *Seven Days a Week: Women and Domestic Service in Industrializing America* (New York: Oxford University Press, 1978).
3. Katzman, *Seven Days*, 53; see also Elizabeth Clark-Lewis, *Living In, Living Out: African American Domestics in Washington D.C., 1910–1940* (Washington: Smithsonian Institute, 2010).
4. Victoria K. Haskins and Claire Lowrie, "Introduction. Decolonizing Domestic Service: Introducing a New Agenda," in *Colonization and*

Domestic Service: Historical and Contemporary Perspectives, ed. Haskins and Lowrie (New York: Routledge, 2015), 5.

5. Rosie Cox, "From Our Own Backyard? Understanding UK Au Pair Policy as Colonial Legacy and Neocolonial Dream," in *Colonization and Domestic Service*, ed. Haskins and Lowrie, 261.

6. Bronwen Walter, "Strangers on the Inside: Irish Women Servants in England, 1881," *Immigrants and Minorities* 27, no. 2–3 (July/November 2009): 279–99; see also McClintock, *Imperial Leather*.

7. Outside the United States, American imperialist ventures in Latin America imported black British Caribbean labour to maintain their households; see Nicola Foote, "British Caribbean Migrants and Domestic Service in Latin America, 1850–1950: Race, Gender and Colonial Legacies," in *Colonization and Domestic Service*, ed. Haskins and Lowrie, 280–308.

8. Palmer, *Domesticity*, 67; Evelyn Nakano Glenn, "From Servitude to Service Work: Historical Continuities in the Racial Division of Paid Reproductive Labor," *Signs* 18, no. 1 (1992): 1–43. For a discussion of capitalism's continuing reliance on migrant labour, see Susan Ferguson and David McNally, "Precarious Migrants: Gender, Race and the Social Reproduction of a Global Working Class," *Socialist Register* (2015).

9. Katzman, *Seven Days*, 62.

10. Ibid., 291–2; Palmer, *Domesticity*, 13, 67 n. 4; Palmer attributes this shift to the dovetailing of black women's preferences and their employers' racist fears of black-white intimacy.

11. Their neglect cannot be explained by a lack of exposure as white and black women were active in both the abolition and suffrage movements; see Teresa Zackodnik, *African American Feminisms 1829–1923* (London: Routledge, 2007).

12. While John Stuart Mill is usually credited with presenting the first sustained critique of women's political exclusion, his work reprises Wheeler's and Thompson's arguments. And although Mill agreed women should not be barred from the occupations, he advocated that they oversee domestic affairs—a position contested by his wife, Harriet Taylor Mill (Rendall, *Origins*, 286–7).

13. Antoinette Brown Blackwell, "Relation of Women's Work in the Household to Work Outside," 1873, in *Up from the Pedestal: Selected Writings in the History of American Feminism*, ed. Aileen S. Kraditor (Chicago: Quadrangle Books, 1975), 151, 155.

14. Frances E. Willard, "How to Win: A Book for Girls," 1888, in *Pedastal*, ed. Kraditor, 318.

15. Charlotte Perkins Gillman, "Economic Basis of the Woman Question," 1898, in *Pedastal*, ed. Kraditor, 176, 177.

16. Ibid., 177–8.

17. Blackwell, "Relation," 156.

18. Charlotte Perkins Gilman, "A Suggestion on the Negro Problem," *The American Journal of Sociology* 14 (July 1908). For an analysis of Perkins Gilman's "racialized reproductive thinking," see Alys Eve Weinbaum,

"Writing Feminist Genealogy: Charlotte Perkins Gilman, Racial National-ism, and the Reproduction of Maternalist Feminism," *Feminist Studies* 27, no. 2 (Summer 2001): 271–302, 271.

19. See Rendall, *Origins*, 316–19; and Delores Hayden, *The Grand Domestic Revolution: A History of Feminist Designs for American Homes, Neighborhoods, and Cities* (Cambridge, MA: MIT Press, 1982).

20. Bebel's book saw 50 editions between 1879 and 1910, with the 1891 9th edition (further revised in 1895) considered a "socialist classic"; see Lise Vogel, *Marxism and the Oppression of Women: Toward a Unitary Theory* (New Brunswick, NJ: Rutgers University Press, 1983), 98. Neither Bebel nor Engels credits Tristan, although Djikstra detects her possible influence on Engels (*Flora Tristan*, 142–7).

21. Friedrich Engels, *The Origin of the Family, Private Property and the State*, 1884 (New York: Pathfinders Press, 1972), 120-1, emphasis in the original.

22. August Bebel, *Woman Under Socialism*, 33rd edition 1904, trans. Daniel De Leon (New York: Schocken Books, 1971), 180, 187, emphasis in the original.

23. According to Engels, the material basis for oppression does not exist within propertyless working class households, although backward ideas linger.

24. Vogel, *Marxism*, 101; Bryson, *Feminist Political Theory*, 61.

25. See Chapter 6. For more recent examples of class reductionist theories, see Tony Cliff, *Class Struggle and Women's Liberation* (London: Bookmarks, 1984); David Harvey, *Seventeen Contradictions and the End of Capitalism* (New York: Oxford University Press, 2014); Ellen Meiksins Wood, *Democracy Against Capitalism: Renewing Historical Materialism* (Cambridge: Cambridge University Press, 1995); Vivek Chibber, "Rescuing Class from the Cultural Turn," *Catalyst* 1, no. 1 (2017).

26. See Philip S. Foner's introduction to *Clara Zetkin: Selected Writings*, Clara Zetkin (New York: International Publishers, 1984), 33–8; and Alix Holt's introduction and commentaries in Alexandra Kollontai, *Selected Writings* (New York: W.W. Norton & Co., 1977), 52–7, 201–2.

27. Zetkin, *Selected Writings*, 45, 46.

28. Kollontai, *Selected Writings*, 63.

29. Zetkin, *Selected Writings*, 77.

30. Kollontai, *Selected Writings*, 60.

31. Ibid., 225. Capitalism's interest in maintaining the family against forces that seek to destroy it, suggests Kollontai, are political—not economic: "For the capitalists are well aware that the old type of family ... constitutes the best weapon in the struggle to stifle the desire of the working class for freedom and to weaken the revolutionary spirit ... The worker is weighed down by his family cares and is obliged to compromise with capital" (257).

32. Ibid., 254.

33. Zetkin, *Selected Writings*, 47. It is unclear here if Zetkin refers to women's social reproductive work or just to home-based industry as she fails to differentiate these in the preceding passage.

34. Ibid., 82.

35. Kollontai, *Selected Writings*, 144, emphasis in the original.

36. Ibid., 134; see also 228.
37. See Vogel for a more fulsome methodological critique of Engels and Bebel (*Marxism*, 73–103).
38. Hayden makes this second argument (*Domestic Revolution*, 5–8).

CHAPTER 5: ANTI-RACIST FEMINISM AND WOMEN'S WORK

1. Although the contributors to this discussion did not identify as feminists, scholars situate them within the "black feminism" tradition; Patricia Hill Collins, *Black Feminist Thought: Knowledge, Consciousness, and the Politics of Empowerment* (New York: Routledge, 2000). I follow this convention while not wanting to homogenize all currents of black feminism, which adhere to—as this chapter shows—divergent and sometimes contradictory positions.
2. Deborah Gray White, *Ar'n't I a Woman? Female Slaves in the Plantation South*, revised edition (W.W. Norton & Co., 1999), 158–85; Jacqueline Jones, *Labor of Love, Labor of Sorrow: Black Women, Work and the Family, from Slavery to the Present*, revised edition (New York: Basic Books, 2010), 26–37.
3. White, *Ar'n't I a Woman*, 123–30.
4. Leslie A. Schwalm, "'Sweet Dreams of Freedom': Freedwomen's Reconstruction of Life and Labor in Lowcountry South Carolina," *Journal of Women's History* 9, no. 1 (1997): 9–38, 10–11.
5. Gerald Jaynes, *Branches Without Roots: Genesis of the Black Working Class in the American South* (New York: Oxford University Press, 1986), 228–33. Although some black feminists encouraged women to become better housekeepers and to "make the homes of the race the shrines of all the domestic virtues rather than a mere shelter." Fannie Barrier Williams, "Club List: Names of the Clubs of the National Association of Colored Women," in *A New Negro for a New Century: An Accurate and Up to Date Record of the Upward Struggles of the Negro Race*, Booker T. Washington, Fannie B. Williams and Norman Barton Wood (Chicago: American Publishing House, 1900), 418.
6. Schwalm, "Sweet Dreams," 11.
7. Jones, *Labor of Love*, 139–43.
8. Collins, *Black Feminist Thought*, 53.
9. Maria W. Stewart, "Religion and the Pure Principles of Morality, the Sure Foundation on Which We Must Build," 1831, in *Words of Fire: An Anthology of African-American Feminist Thought*, ed. Beverly Guy-Sheftall (New York: New Press, 1995), 29.
10. Maria Stewart, "Maria Stewart Calls for the Upliftment of her Race," 1932, in *Women at the Podium: Memorable Speeches in History*, introduction by S. Michele Nix (New York: HarperCollins, 2000), 101.
11. Stewart, "Religion," 30.
12. Sojourner Truth, "When Woman Gets her Rights Man will be Right," 1867, in *Words of Fire*, ed. Guy-Sheftall, 37.

13. Racial uplift was a central concern of the black women's "club movement." Bryson reports that in 1896, 50,000 black women were members of 1000 mutual aid, social reform, and "improvement" societies (*Feminist Political Theory*, 74). For an overview, see Anne Firor Scott, "Most Invisible of All: Black Women's Voluntary Associations," *The Journal of Southern History* 56, no. 1 (1990): 2–22.

14. Cooper wrote her book and many articles and speeches before completing her doctorate at the Sorbonne University in Paris in 1924.

15. Mrs. N.F. [Gertrude] Mossell, *The Work of the Afro-American Woman* (Philadelphia: Geo S. Ferguson Company, 1894), 24.

16. Guy-Sheftall, *Words of Fire*, 8–11.

17. Anna Julia Cooper, *A Voice from the South* (Xenia, OH: The Aldine Printing House, 1892), 130.

18. Ibid.

19. Stewart, "Religion," 28.

20. Cooper, *A Voice*, 71.

21. Williams, "Club List," 417.

22. Stewart, "Upliftment," 100; Stewart did, however, note that a life in service was acceptable for those whose "inclination leads them to aspire no higher" (102).

23. Cooper, *A Voice*, 254.

24. Wollstonecraft, *Vindication*, 232; see Chapter 2.

25. Guy-Sheftall, *Words of Fire*, 79.

26. Elise Johnson McDougald, "The Struggle of Negro Women for Sex and Race Emancipation," 1925, in *Words of Fire*, ed. Guy-Sheftall, 81.

27. Sadie Tanner Alexander, "Negro Women in Our Economic Life," 1930, in *Words of Fire*, ed. Guy-Sheftall, 99, 96.

28. Ibid., 100.

29. Ibid., 99, 98. She also points to women's high turnover rate because they leave the workforce to have children.

30. Ibid., 98.

31. Bill Mullen, "The Russian Revolution, Black Bolshevichki and Social Reproduction," *Viewpoint Magazine* (December 14, 2017), www.viewpointmag.com/2017/12/14/russian-revolution-black-bolshevichki-social-reproduction/.

32. Louise Thompson Patterson, "Toward a Brighter Dawn," *Woman Today* (April 1936), reprinted in *Viewpoint Magazine* (October 31, 2015), www.viewpointmag.com/2015/10/31/toward-a-brighter-dawn-1936/; see also Erik S. McDuffie, *Sojourning for Freedom: Black Women, American Communism and the Making of Black Left Feminism* (Durham, NC: Duke University Press, 2011), 112.

33. US authorities jailed and eventually deported Jones for her political activism. See McDuffie, *Sojourning*, for a full account. For a useful summary, see Carole Boyce Davies' introduction to Claudia Jones, "We Seek Full Equality for Women," 1949, *Viewpoint Magazine* (February 21, 2015), www.viewpointmag.com/2015/02/21/we-seek-full-equality-for-women/.

34. Claudia Jones, "An End to the Neglect of the Problems of the Negro Woman!" *Political Affairs* (June 1949): 3–19, 7.

35. Ibid., 5, 16–17, emphasis added.

36. Jones, "We Seek", emphasis in the original.

37. Jones, "An End," 15–16.

38. Jones points to the committee to defend Rosa Lee Ingram as an example of a civil rights struggle that socialists should support. She argues that support for Ingram—a black woman from Georgia sentenced to life imprisonment for "defending herself from the indecent advances of a 'white supremacist'"—is "a prime necessity for all progressives." See ibid., 15, 16.

39. Ibid., 5.

40. Ibid., 3–4, 9.

41. Jones, "We Seek."

42. Mullen, "The Russian Revolution."

CHAPTER 6: A POLITICAL ECONOMY OF "WOMEN'S WORK": PRODUCING PATRIARCHAL CAPITALISM

1. Some (maternalist) equality feminists argue instead for equal but separate forms of work, advocating women's moral (rather than economic) autonomy. They tend to emphasize improving the conditions of unpaid domestic work, rather than escaping it. For a discussion of the convergence of this approach with imperialist aspirations and racism, see Cecile Devereaux, "New Woman, New World: Maternal Feminism and the New Imperialism in the White Settler Colonies," *Women's Studies International Forum* 2, no. 2 (1999): 175–84.

2. I say "may be" because some within this tradition propose it is in fact "productive"—a distinction I address below.

3. Some CPUSA socialist feminists were unconvinced, pointing out that women were no better off when burdened with both waged and unwaged work; see Grace Hutchins, "Women Under Capitalism," and Rebecca Pitts, "Women and Communism," in *Writing Red: An Anthology of American Women Writers, 1930–1940*, ed. Charlotte Nekola and Paula Robinowitz (New York: Feminist Press of the City University of New York, 1987).

4. Charlotte Nekola, "Worlds Unseen: Political Women Journalists and the 1930s," in *Writing Red*, ed. Nekola and Robinowitz, 196.

5. Inman's 1942 book, *Woman Power*, in which she develops her argument in a more focused and sustained manner, is even harder to find. A 1964 pamphlet, *The Two Forms of Production Under Capitalism*, however, recaps much of what appears in *Woman Power*. I draw here on a close reading of *In Woman's Defense* informed by her pamphlet and secondary sources. See Clark A. Pomerleau, *Califia Women: Feminist Education Against Sexism, Classism, and Racism* (Austin: University of Texas Press, 2013).

6. Mary Inman, *In Woman's Defense* (Los Angeles: The Committee to Organize the Advancement of Women, 1940), 23, 137, 135.

7. Ibid., 136, 34, 133.

8. Ibid., 149.

9. Ibid.

10. Ibid., 59, 102, 138. By 1964, she reverses this position, and stresses the cross-class nature of women's reproductive labour; see Mary Inman, *The Two Forms of Production Under Capitalism* (Long Beach, CA: Mary Inman, 1964), 34.

11. Inman, *Woman's Defense*, 170, 171.

12. Ibid., 34. The "credit" Inman has in mind is not monetary but moral: she wants the value of women's unpaid labour to be acknowledged, to encourage housewives to organize.

13. Ibid., 137, emphasis in the original.

14. Inman's claim that unpaid domestic work is "productive" and that the value of women's labour is reflected in the wage (see *Two Forms* 16, 29–30) are among her weakest points.

15. For an account of the "Mary Inman Controversy," see Kate Weigand, *Red Feminism: American Communism and the Making of Women's Liberation* (Baltimore: Johns Hopkins University Press, 2000), 34–40. For a more critical view of the CPUSA leadership's role than Weigand allows, see Rebecca Hill, "Review Essay. Re-evaluating the CPUSA's Answer to the Woman Question," *American Communist History* 3, no. 1 (2004): 145–51.

16. A. Landy, *Marxism and the Woman Question* (New York: Worker Library Publishers, 1943), 8. Landy is responding to Inman's more theoretically developed book *Woman Power* (see n. 5 above).

17. Landy, *Marxism*, 14.

18. Ibid., 18. For her rebuttal, see Mary Inman, "13 Years of CPUSA Misleadership on the Woman Question," 1949, Encyclopedia of Anti-Revisionism On-Line, Marxist Internet Archive, www.marxists.org/history/erol/1946-1956/inman.htm.

19. Pomerleau, *Califia Women*, 101; Weigand, *Red Feminism*, 37–40.

20. Hill, "Review Essay," 147–9.

21. For a considered appraisal of Friedan's work and impact, see Stephanie Coontz, *A Strange Stirring: The Feminine Mystique and American Women at the Dawn of the 1960s* (New York: Basic Books, 2011).

22. Chinhui Juhn and Simon Potter, "Changes in Labor Force Participation in the United States," *Journal of Economic Perspectives* 20, no. 3 (Summer 2006): 27–46; Howard N. Fullerton Jr., "Labor Force Participation: 74 Years of Change, 1950–1998 and 1998–2025," *Monthly Labor Review* (December 1999), Bureau of Labor Statistics, https://www.bls.gov/mlr/1999/12/art1full.pdf.

23. Jones, *Labor of Love*, 244–51.

24. Coontz, *Strange Stirring*, 5–15.

25. Betty Friedan, *The Feminine Mystique*, 1963 (New York: W.W. Norton & Co, 2001), 358. Friedan does not seem to have menial or service labour in mind when she counsels women to find jobs that give purpose to the future.

26. Black feminist civil rights activist and lawyer Pauli Murray is sometimes credited with co-authoring the Statement. NOW's website lists Friedan alone as author, however Coontz writes that Friedan "with Pauli Murray, helped develop" it (*Strange Stirring*, 157). Murray, who is better known for pushing lawmakers to include protection against gender-based (as well as race-based) workplace discrimination in the Civil Rights Act, resigned from NOW shortly after its founding because she objected to its narrow focus on "well-educated suburban women and women professionals" (Jones, *Labor of Love*, 252); see also Sarah Azaransky, "Jane Crow: Pauli Murray's Intersections and Antidiscrimination Law," Roundtable Embodying Radical Democracy, *Journal of Feminist Studies in Religion* 29, no. 1: 155–60.

27. "NOW's 1966 Statement of Purpose," National Organization for Women Blog, https://350fem.blogs.brynmawr.edu/about/statement-of-purpose/.

28. See Nancy Fraser, *From Fortunes of Feminism: From State-Managed Capitalism to Neoliberal Crisis* (Brooklyn, NY: Verso Books, 2013); and Adrienne Roberts, "The Political Economy of 'Transnational Business Feminism': Problematizing the Corporate Led Gender Equality Agenda," *International Feminist Journal of Politics* 17, no. 2 (2014): 209–31.

29. Inman, *Woman's Defense*, 58.

30. Inman, *Two Forms*, 35, n.5.

31. See Premilla Nadasen, *Rethinking the Welfare Rights Movement* (London: Routledge, 2012).

32. Meg Luxton and Pat Armstrong, "Margaret Lowe Benston: 1937–1991," *Studies in Political Economy* 35, no. 1 (1991): 7–11, 7. Benston later taught Women's Studies and Computer Science.

33. Benston references not Inman but Juliet Mitchell's 1966 *New Left Review* article, "Women the Longest Revolution"; see Margaret Benston, "The Political Economy of Women's Liberation," *Monthly Review* (September 1969), 13–27, 17. For more on Benston's life and work, see Ellen Balka, "Obituary. Margaret Lowe Benston, 1937–1991," *Labour/Le Travail* 28 (Fall 1991): 11–13; and Angela Miles, "Margaret Benston's 'Political Economy of Women's Liberation': International Impact," *Canadian Women's Studies/Les cahiers de la femme* 13, no. 2 (1993): 31–5.

34. Benston, "Political Economy," 18.

35. Ibid., 23, 15.

36. Ibid., 16, 21.

37. Ibid., 23. Benston's insistence that women "are not merely discriminated against; [they] are exploited" (24) is an example of how confusing it can be to redraw the Marxist theoretical paradigm. Clearly, because she does not see unpaid labour as capitalistically "productive," housewives are not capitalistically "exploited" (they do not directly produce more value than is returned to them as wages). At the same time, capitalists are getting something for free and therefore exploitation (in its more generic sense) is occurring. Terminological clarity is an abiding problem, one we continue to see in disagreement about "productive" labour (see Chapter 7).

38. Mariarosa Dalla Costa and Christine Delphy published articles making related arguments in Italian and French around the same time; see Louise Toupin, *Wages for Housework: A History of an International Feminist Movement, 1972–77*, trans. Käthe Roth (Vancouver: UBC Press, 2018).

39. See Vogel, *Marxism*, 13–37.

40. Pat Mainardi, "The Politics of Housework," 1969, Caring Labor: An Archive (September 11, 2010), https://caringlabor.wordpress.com/2010/09/11/pat-mainardi-the-politics-of-housework/. Mainardi wrote the article as a "seed paper" for Redstockings, of which she was a founding member. It was reprinted in Robin Morgan's *Sisterhood is Powerful* in 1970; "Consciousness-Raising and Pro-Women Line Papers, 1968–72," Redstockings, www.redstockings.org/index.php/main/consciousness-raising-papers-1968-72.

41. Cited in Carol Hanisch, "Housework, Reproduction and Women's Liberation," Meeting Ground: For the Liberation of Women and Working People, http://meetinggroundonline.org/housework-reproduction-and-womens-liberation-2/.

42. Toupin, *Wages*, 3; see also Rada Katsarova, "Repression and Resistance on the Terrain of Social Reproduction: Historical Trajectories, Contemporary Openings," *Viewpoint Magazine* (October 31, 2015), www.viewpointmag.com/2015/10/31/repression-and-resistance-on-the-terrain-of-social-reproduction-historical-trajectories-contemporary-openings/; and Laura Ranata Martin, "'All the Work We Do as Women' Feminist Manifestos on Prostitution and the States 1977, Introductory Text," *LIES*, vol. 1 (2016).

43. Silvia Federici, *Revolution at Point Zero: Housework, Reproduction, and Feminist Struggle* (Oakland, CA: PM Press, 2012), 17.

44. Their analysis drew on and influenced the autonomist Marxist tradition (see Chapter 8).

45. Mariarosa Dalla Costa and Selma James, *Sex, Race and Class* (Bristol: Falling Wall Press, 1972), Upping the Anti, https://uppingtheanti.org/journal/article/01-sex-race-and-class.

46. See Weeks, *Problem with Work*, 128–36 for an excellent interpretation of the WfH demand as a political perspective.

47. Federici, *Revolution*, 19–20.

48. Toupin, *Wages*, 46. See page 4 for a summary list of feminist objections to WfH.

49. Melissa Benn, "A Most Unshowy Icon," *Guardian* (October 21, 2008). Rowbotham made headlines in 2008 because an international campaign had secured her reinstatement at Manchester University where, at 65, she was expected to accept a forced retirement quietly.

50. Sheila Rowbotham, *Woman's Consciousness, Man's World* (Harmondsworth: Penguin, 1973), 63, emphasis added.

51. Ibid., 123, 64–5.

52. Ibid., 66.

53. Ibid. By "point of procreation" she seems to mean the site of the family, and not simply the processes involved in childbirth.

54. The WfH campaign logic does not apply: although housework is essential to capitalism, it does not contribute directly to the creation of surplus value, making its claim on a wage less certain. Moreover, Rowbotham stresses that women are groomed to be caretakers, a fact which means they might resist entering the cash-nexus in any case.

55. Ibid., 101, 100.

56. Ibid., 125.

57. I use the term "extra-economic" with some reservation because gender, race, and other oppressions are also "economic" in nature.

58. See, for example, Wood, *Democracy Against Capitalism*; and Harvey, *Seventeen Contradictions*.

59. David McNally, "The Dual Form of Labour in Capitalist Society and the Struggle over Meaning: Comments on Postone," *Historical Materialism* 12, no. 3 (2010): 189–208, 198.

60. Cited in Toupin, *Wages*, 54–5; although James and Dalla Costa are broadly concerned with wagelessness, they see the specifically *feminist* issue as one of housework.

61. Rowbotham, *Woman's Consciousness*, 32, 67.

62. Angela Davis, *Women, Race, and Class* (New York: Vintage Books, 1981), 229, 237.

63. Chandra Talpade Mohanty, "Under Western Eyes: Feminist Scholarship and Colonial Discourses," *Boundary* 212, no. 3 (1986): 333–58. Mohanty revisits and updates this seminal article in "'Under Western Eyes' Revisited: Feminist Solidarity and Anticapitalist Struggles," *Signs* 28, no. 2 (Winter 2003): 499–535.

64. Federici, *Revolution*, 33.

65. Selma James, ed., *Strangers and Sisters: Women, Race & Immigration* (Bristol: Falling Wall Press, 1985), 12.

66. Dalla Costa and James, *Sex, Race and Class*.

67. For an excellent overview of the theoretical obfuscations, see Cinzia Arruzza, "Functionalist, Determinist, Reductionist: Social Reproduction Feminism and its Critics," *Science & Society* 80, no. 1 (January 2016): 9–30. I agree with Arruzza's conclusion that "functionism is not an intrinsic weakness of the concept of social reproduction, but rather the outcome of the difficulty socialist and Marxist feminists had in articulating social reproduction into a consistent theory" (27).

68. Some of those involved in promoting "materialist feminism" in the 1980s and 1990s represent an important exception to this general trend. See Rosemary Hennessey, *Materialist Feminism and the Politics of Discourse* (New York: Routledge, 1993).

CHAPTER 7: RENEWING SOCIAL REPRODUCTION FEMINISM

1. Dionne Brand, "A Working Paper on Black Women in Toronto: Gender, Race and Class," in *Returning the Gaze: Essays on Racism, Feminism and Politics*, ed. Himani Bannerji (Toronto: Sister Vision Press, 1993), 224.

Thanks to Mary Jo Nadeau for drawing my attention to this passage. Nadeau shared with me her MA thesis—completed at York University in 1995, under the supervision of Himani Bannerji—just as I was beginning to write this chapter. In it she expertly analyzes two classic works of Canadian social reproduction feminism, arguing that they adopt a "concealed standpoint" of white middle class women by centering their analyses around unpaid housework; see Dorothy E. Smith, "Feminist Reflections on Political Economy," *Studies in Political Economy* 30, no. 1 (1989): 37–59, 55.

2. For a methodological critique of socialist feminist political economy, see Smith "Feminist Reflections" and Himani Bannerji, "But Who Speaks for Us? Experience and Agency in Conventional Feminist Paradigms," in *Thinking Through: Essays on Feminism, Marxism, and Anti-Racism*, ed. Bannerji (Toronto: Women's Press, 1995).

3. Their name derives from an 1863 Union Army raid along the Combahee River led by Harriet Tubman that freed 750 enslaved black men and women; see Helen Leichner, "Combahee River Raid (June 2, 1863)," Blackpast (December 21, 2012), www.blackpast.org/african-american-history/combahee-river-raid-june-2-1863/. For a discussion of the CRC origins based on interviews with three founding members, see Keeanga-Yamahtta Taylor, ed., *How We Get Free: Black Feminism and the Combahee River Collective* (Chicago: Haymarket Books, 2017).

4. Taylor, *How We Get Free*, 60, 124.

5. The Statement was later published as "A Black Feminist Statement," in Zillah Eisenstein's *Capitalist Patriarchy and the Case for Socialist Feminism* (New York: Monthly Review Press, 1979).

6. Kristen A. Kolenz et al., "Combahee River Collective Statement: A Fortieth Anniversary Retrospective," *Frontiers: A Journal of Women's Studies* 38, no. 3 (2017): 164–89, 170.

7. Taylor, *How We Get Free*, 69; see also 50.

8. "The Women of the Combahee River Collective," Combahee River Collective, https://combaheerivercollective.weebly.com/, emphasis added.

9. Taylor, *How We Get Free*, 102.

10. Stewart, "Religion," 29.

11. Jones, "An End," 17.

12. See Jones, *Labor of Love*, 256–65.

13. Davis had taught philosophy at UCLA when then-governor Ronald Reagan had tried (and failed) to get her fired for her membership in the CPUSA. She was later imprisoned for sixteen months on a conspiracy to commit murder charge. The Free Angela Davis campaign won international support, and she was eventually acquitted.

14. Davis, *Women, Race, and Class*, 234.

15. Ibid., 236–8.

16. David McNally, "Dual Form," 109.

17. Those who did grapple with it tended to abandon the socialist feminist explanations discussed here, embracing either intersectionality feminism or retreating from materialist frameworks all together. See Arruzza,

"Functionalist"; see also Susan Ferguson and David McNally, "Capital, Labour-Power, and Gender-Relations: Introduction to the *Historical Materialism Edition of Marxism and the Oppression of Women*," in Lise Vogel's *Marxism and the Oppression of Women: Toward a Unitary Theory*, 2nd edition (Chicago: Haymarket Books, 2013).

18. Hazel V. Carby, "White Woman Listen! Black Feminism and the Boundaries of Sisterhood," Northern Arizona University, https://jan.ucc.nau.edu/~sj6/carby%20white%20woman%20listen.pdf, 118. Carby's article was originally published in *The Empire Strikes Back: Race and Racism in 70s Britain*, ed. Carby and Paul Gilroy, 1982 (London: Routledge, 2004).

19. *This Bridge Called My Back* (New York: Kitchen Table Press, 1981) by Cheríe Moraga and Gloria Anzaldúa expanded upon and deepened the CRC perspective. Kimberlé Crenshaw and Patricia Hill Collins each developed the perspective in distinct directions. For different interpretations of its legacy, see Jennifer C. Nash, "Re-thinking Intersectionality," *Feminist Review* 89 (2008): 1–15; Leslie McCall, "The Complexity of Intersectionality," *Signs* 30, no. 3 (2005): 1771–800; and Sirma Bilge, "Intersectionality Undone: Saving Intersectionality from Feminist Intersectionality Studies," *Du Bois Review* 10, no. 2 (2013): 405–24.

20. See my "Intersectionality and Social Reproduction Feminisms: Toward an Integrative Ontology," *Historical Materialism* 24, no. 2 (2016): 38–60; see also Shahrzad Mojab and Sara Carpenter, "Marxism, Feminism, and 'Intersectionality,'" *Journal of Labor and Society* 22, no. 2 (June 2019): 275–82; and David McNally, "Intersections and Dialectics: Critical Reconstructions in Social Reproduction Theory," in *Social Reproduction Theory: Remapping Class, Recentering Oppression*, ed. Tithi Bhattacharya (London: Pluto Press, 2017). See McNally also for a discussion of the importance of such critical appropriation in developing an ever more richly concrete comprehension of people's particular and shared experiences of the world.

21. Johanna Brenner, *Women and the Politics of Class* (New York: Monthly Review Press, 2000), 86.

22. For a discussion of Canadian social reproduction feminism of this period, see my "Building on the Strengths of the Socialist Feminist Tradition," *Critical Sociology* 25, no. 1 (1999): 1–15.

23. Marx, *Capital*, 270. See Ferguson and McNally, "Precarious Migrants," 4–5 for a critique of Marx's (flawed) explanation of the production of labour power. See also our "Capital, Labour-Power" (xxiii–xxvi) for an expanded discussion of Vogel's important contribution.

24. I discuss the debate over understanding social reproductive labour as capitalistically "productive" or not in Chapter 8.

25. Vogel, *Marxism*, 156.

26. Ibid., 129, emphasis in the original.

27. Ibid.

28. Ibid., 171.

29. Ibid., 152.

30. This is the same dynamic of dispossession and primitive accumulation involved in the transition from feudalism to capitalism (see Chapter 1).

31. Federici, *Caliban*, 17.

32. See Chapter 5.

33. See, for example, Isabella Bakker and Rachel Silvey, eds., *Beyond States and Markets: The Challenges of Social Reproduction* (New York: Routledge, 2008); and Ferguson and McNally, "Precarious Migrants."

34. Capitalism is widely seen as a system of "free" labour, as opposed to slavery or feudalism where workers are bonded to owners or employers. Marx takes issue with that characterization, pointing out the economic coercion capitalism entails (one is not free if one has no choice but to work in order to live; see Chapter 1). Jairus Banaji expands that critique, suggesting that capitalist labour is better characterized by varying degrees of unfreedom; see Jairus Banaji, "The Fictions of Free Labour: Contract, Coercion and So-called Unfree Labour," *Historical Materialism* 11, no. 3 (2003): 69–95; see also Genevieve LeBaron, "Unfree Labor Beyond Binaries: Social Hierarchy, Insecurity, and Labor Market Restructuring," *International Feminist Journal of Politics* 17, no. 1 (2015), 1–19; and Todd Gordon, "Capitalism, Neoliberalism and Unfree Labour," *Critical Sociology* (April 20, 2018), doi.org/10.1177/0896920518763936.

35. See "Migration Data Portal: The Bigger Picture," International Organization for Migration (2019), https://migrationdataportal.org/themes/international-migration-flows.

36. Federici, *Revolution*, 71.

37. Alessandra Mezzadri, *The Sweatshop Regime: Labouring Bodies, Exploitation, and Garments Made in India* (New York: Cambridge University Press, 2017), 5, 37.

38. Ibid., 134.

39. Federici, *Revolution*, 104. Yet, she also notes that capital is never completely indifferent to the loss of life since it cannot exist without living labour.

CHAPTER 8: THE SOCIAL REPRODUCTION STRIKE: LIFE-MAKING BEYOND CAPITALISM

1. See Maya Gonzalez, "The Gendered Circuit: Reading The Arcane of Reproduction," *Viewpoint Magazine* (September 28, 2013), www.viewpointmag.com/2013/09/28/the-gendered-circuit-reading-the-arcane-of-reproduction/.

2. See Steve Wright, *Storming Heaven: Class Composition and Struggle in Italian Autonomist Marxism* (London: Pluto Press, 2002).

3. Other early theorists associated with this tradition include Antonio Negri, Félix Guattari, and Adriano Sofri.

4. Federici, *Revolution*, 35.

5. The latter was seen not so much as undesirable but as insufficient. State-provided daycare, for instance, does not necessarily challenge (and may reinforce) the gender division of labour.

6. Dalla Costa and James, *Power of Women*, 20. See Chapter 6 for more on the WfH campaign.

7. The Marxian school is not an explicitly organized group or "school." The designation is entirely my own, based on my understanding of those who share a theoretical and political perspective; I use it here to meet my need for a succinct way of referring to socialist feminists, like myself, who have been influenced by Lise Vogel's work. I call it "Marxian" not to lay exclusive claim to Marx's mantle, but to emphasize our close adherence to Marx's theory of value.

8. The exception is paid social reproductive labour performed in for-profit enterprises, such as private schools, childcare centers, or restaurants. In these cases, the product of social reproductive labour *is* exchanged on the market (even as it also produces labour power).

9. Leopoldina Fortunati, *The Arcane of Reproduction: Housework, Prostitution, Labor and Capital*, 1981, trans. Hilary Creek and ed. Jim Fleming (Brooklyn, NY: Autonomedia, 1995), 9. Fortunati was active in Italian workerist and feminist struggles in the 1970s, eventually joining *Lotta Femminista* in which she worked with Dalla Costa and others on the WfH campaign. See also Fortunati, "Learning to Struggle: My Story Between Workerism and Feminism," *Viewpoint Magazine* (September 15, 2013), www.viewpointmag. com/2013/09/15/learning-to-struggle-my-story-between-workerism-and-feminism/. Gonzalez calls *The Arcane* (published in 1981 in Italian and 1995 in English), "one of the most important Marxist contributions to a theory of gendered exploitation, and also one of the most widely misunderstood" ("Gendered Circuit").

10. Fortunati, *Arcane*, 105, emphasis added.

11. This is not to say that *all* social reproductive labour is "unproductive" (see n. 8 above).

12. Indeed, some criticize the Marxian school for being overly beholden to Marxist orthodoxy. See Alessandra Mezzadri, "On the Value of Social Reproduction: Informal Labour, the Majority World, and the Need for Inclusive Theory and Politics," *Radical Philosophy* 2, no. 4 (Spring 2019), https://www.radicalphilosophy.com/article/on-the-value-of-social-reproduction; and Weeks, *Problem with Work*, 244, n. 12.

13. Dalla Costa and James, *Power of Women*, 16, n. 12.

14. This conceptual confusion is repeated and elaborated upon in social reproduction feminist analyses of digital media. See, for example, Kylie Jarrett, "The Relevance of 'Women's Work': Social Reproduction and Immaterial Labor in Digital Media," *Television & New Media* 15, no. 1 (2014): 14–29.

15. It excludes social reproductive labour in the private sector (such as cooks in restaurants or teachers in private schools), which is in fact "productive" labour because its products while also sustaining life (restaurant meals,

education) are produced to be sold on the capitalist market (see n. 8 above). Marx applies this rationale to the teaching profession: "A schoolmaster who educates others is not a productive worker. But a schoolmaster who is engaged as a wage labourer in an institution along with others, in order through his labour to valorise the money of the entrepreneur of the *knowledge-mongering institution*, is a productive worker"; see Karl Marx and Frederick Engels, *Economic Works of Karl Marx, 1861–1864*, vol. 34, trans. Ben Fowkes (London: Lawrence & Wishart, 1994), 484.

16. Those whose spaces of social reproduction and waged work overlap (live-in caregivers or migrant workers housed in employer-owned camps, for instance) have considerably less flexibility in this regard.

17. See D.E. Mulcahy, D.G. Mulcahy and Roger Saul, eds., *Education in North America* (London: Bloomsbury, 2014).

18. For an example of the positive spin placed on this development, where technology is cited as improving efficiency *and* engagement, see "Technology and the Workforce of the Future: The Future of Work in Healthcare," Deloitte.com, www2.deloitte.com/us/en/pages/life-sciences-and-health-care/articles/healthcare-workforce-technology.html. For a more critical view, see Eileen Boris and Rhacel Salazar Perrenas, eds., *Intimate Labors: Cultures, Technologies and the Politics of Care* (Stanford, CA: Stanford University Press, 2010).

19. Ursula Huws makes this point about capitalistically "productive" labour in the creative industries as well; see her *Labor in the Global Digital Economy: The Cybertariat Comes of Age* (New York: Monthly Review Press, 2014).

20. For an excellent examination of how such proxies have been imposed in the higher education sector, see Eric Newstadt, *The Value of Quality: Capital, Class, and Quality Assessment in the Re-making of Higher Education in the United States, the United Kingdom, and Ontario*, PhD Dissertation, York University, Toronto (December 23, 2013).

21. See McNally, "Dual Form."

22. Federici, *Revolution*, 99.

23. Ibid., 111, emphasis added.

24. Matthew Carlin and Silvia Federici, "The Exploitation of Women, Social Reproduction, and the Struggle Against Global Capital," *Theory & Event* (January 2014), https://www.researchgate.net/publication/303289331_The_Exploitation_of_Women_Social_Reproduction_and_the_Struggle_against_Global_Capital: 2.

25. George Caffentzis and Silvia Federici, "Commons Against and Beyond Capitalism," *Community Development Journal* 49, no. 51 (January 2014): 92–105, 100.

26. Weeks, *Problem with Work*, 90, 25, 158. The "productivist" conception of human life and society Weeks takes issue with is elaborated in Chapter 1.

27. Ibid., 103, emphasis added, 168. While Weeks advocates demanding a "sufficient, unconditional and continuous" (138) UBI that does not replace existing social services, John Clarke argues that no contemporary government would pass such a policy, and for the left to endorse UBI is

to grant legitimacy to the neoliberal agenda that will use UBI as a means of clawing back social services and offloading state responsibilities onto individuals. See John Clarke, *Basic Income in the Neo-liberal Age* (Toronto: Socialist Project, 2017).

28. Weeks, *Problem with Work*, 149.

29. Arruzza et al., *Feminism*, Thesis 1.

30. Referring to the recent wave of teachers strikes in the United States, Kate Doyle Griffiths proposes that certain sites of paid social reproductive labour constitute "choke points" of resistance to capital in the same way that Kim Moody argues the capitalistically "productive" logistics industry is. See Griffiths, "Queer Workers, Social Reproduction and Left Strategy" (November 19, 2018), www.patreon.com/posts/queer-workers-22819890; and Moody, *On New Terrain: How Capital is Reshaping the Battleground of Class War* (Chicago: Haymarket, 2017).

31. Tithi Bhattacharya, "Why the Teachers' Revolt Must Confront Racism Head On," *Dissent* (May 1, 2018), www.dissentmagazine.org/online_articles/why-teachers-strikes-must-confront-racism.

32. Ginger Adams Otis, "N.Y. Teamsters for 'Sanctuary Union' to Fight ICE Agents," *Daily News* (February 10, 2018), www.nydailynews.com/new-york/n-y-teamsters-form-sanctuary-union-fight-ice-agents-article-1.3813201.

33. Arruzza et al., *Feminism*, Postface 1.

34. Eric Blanc, *Red State Revolt: The Teachers' Strikes and Working-Class Politics* (London: Verso, 2019), 3.

35. Ibid., 41.

36. Kate Doyle Griffiths, "Crossroads and Country Roads: Wildcat West Virginia and the Possibilities of a Working Class Offensive," *Viewpoint Magazine* (March 13, 2018), www.viewpointmag.com/2018/03/13/crossroads-and-country-roads-wildcat-west-virginia-and-the-possibilities-of-a-working-class-offensive/.

37. Blanc, *Red State*, 64–7, 81–2.

38. Arruzza et al., *Feminism*, Thesis 10.

39. Caffentzis and Federici, "Commons," 102.

40. Weeks, *Problem with Work*, 149.

41. To be clear, the Marxian school suggests no labour exists outside of capitalist domination, but *not* all labour within capitalism is fully subsumed to the logic of accumulation. Autonomist Marxist feminism suggests that it is possible to build alternatives to capitalism, but that all labour within capitalism *is* fully subsumed to its logic.

42. For Marx, producer cooperatives could play a progressive role in the transition to capitalism but are also subject to certain limitations. See Bruno Jossa, "Marx, Marxism and the Cooperative Movement," *Cambridge Journal of Economics* 29 (2005): 3–18.

43. Arruzza et al., *Feminism*, Thesis 10.

44. Ibid., Thesis 6. Solidarity here should not be equated with universal sisterhood, as the latter denies the determinative influences of capitalist oppressions and exploitation.

Index

utopian socialist feminism, 23–4, 35–6, 40, 56–7, 146
  see also Cooperation; *Saint-Simoniennes*; Thompson, William; Tristan, Flora; Wheeler, Anna

value theory, debates, 6, 119, 121–6
  see also Domestic Labour Debate
Vindication of the Rights of Man, A, 32
Vindication of the Rights of Woman, A, 31–5, 44, 55
  see also Wollstonecraft, Mary
Vogel, Lise, 6, 107, 126
  theoretical contributions, 110–14
Voice from the South, A
  see Cooper, Anna Julia
Voilquin, Suzanne
  see Saint-Simoniennes

Wages Against Housework, 97
  see also Federici, Silvia
Wages for Housework campaign, 5, 85, 96–8, 121, 132
  criticisms of, 98, 103, 109
Wakefield, Priscilla, 37–8
"We Seek Full Equality for Women", 79
  see also Jones, Claudia
Weeks, Kathi, 55
  anti-capitalist resistance, 131–2, 133, 136–7
  see also Universal Basic Income
Wheeler, Anna, 3, 40–9, 55–9, 68, 87, 98, 113, 120
  gender division of labour, 150; productivism, 42, 55–7; relation with William Thompson, 150; theoretical contributions, 40–1, 44–7, 57
  see also Owen, Robert; political-economic critique of labour
White, Deborah Gray, 73
"White Woman Listen!"
  see Carby, Hazel

Willard, Frances, 62
Williams, Fannie Barrier, 75
Winstanley, Gerrard, 26, 146
Wollstonecraft, Mary, 3, 23, 44, 48, 55, 58
  economic theory of, 31–6, 148; education, women's, 31, 33–4; egalitarianism, 31, 34; Flora Tristan and, 52–3; misogyny, 147; *querelle des femmes* and, 35–6; theoretical contributions, 30–6
Woman and Socialism
  see Bebel, August
Woman's Consciousness, Man's World, 96
  see also Rowbotham, Sheila
Woman's Labour, The, 28
  see also Collier, Mary
Women and Economics
  see Perkins, Charlotte Gilman
Women, Race, and Class, 109
  see also Davis, Angela
Womens Sharpe Revenge, The, 26
Women's Social and Political Union, 62
Women's Strikes, 1–2
  see also Feminism for the 99%
women's work, 143
  see also domestic labour, paid; domestic labour, unpaid; gender division of labour; labour; social reproductive labour
Work of the Afro-American Woman, The
  see Mossell, Gertrude
Wright, Melissa, 118

Yearsley, Ann Cromartie, 29–30, 39
Young, Iris, 111

Zaretsky, Eli, 111
Zetkin, Clara, 4, 69, 71, 89, 154
  theoretical contributions, 65–8

The Pluto Press Newsletter

Hello friend of Pluto!

Want to stay on top of the best radical books we publish?

Then sign up to be the first to hear about our new books, as well as special events, podcasts and videos.

You'll also get 50% off your first order with us when you sign up.

Come and join us!

Go to bit.ly/PlutoNewsletter